Monographic Journals of the Near East   *Afroasiatic Linguistics* 8/1 (May 1981)

T0153734

MORPHOPHONEMICS OF THE VERB IN RENDI

by

Ronald J. Sim,
Nairobi, Kenya

The morphology and morphophonemics of the verb in Rendille are treated; of simple stems consisting of a bare root, and of derived stems consisting of a root plus an extension affix. Suffix extensions—which may be reflexive-middle, causative, agentive—are dealt with in some detail; brief mention is made of prefix extensions, in particular the reduplicative. Some notes are included on verbal noun forms. Morphophonemic alternations in the verb are examined. Attention is drawn to the primacy of a 2-Consonant constraint in Rendille and various rule conspiracies designed to prevent violations of this; and rule conspiracies; phonotactically constrained consonant metathesis and a 'peeking rule'.

Table of Contents

---

[1] The Rendille, some 15,000-18,000 strong, live in southern Marsabit district in north Kenya. The language is East Cushitic, and is grouped by Heine (1976) with Somali and Aweera (Boni) to form the "Eastern Omo-Tana" languages.

1. INTRODUCTION

This study[2] was prompted by two considerations. First, Heine (1976) was available during a study of Konso verbal morphophonemics (Sim, 1977a), and similarities of pattern in the two languages inspired interest as well as suggesting lines of analysis which Heine had not developed. Secondly, neither Heine (1976) nor Oomen (1977) appeared to record gemination of segments in the verb nor to commit themselves to recognizing a benefactive or reflexive-middle formative,[3] both of which features are important in Konso for the elucidation of generalizations, and this too influenced the decision to examine the Rendille verb with attention to just those details.[4]

---

[2] The research was carried out in Nairobi during November 1977 while I was engaged in work with Summer Institute of Linguistics. Bernhard Barchuma Arbele was my language informant. I am grateful to Mrs. Antoinette Oomen for this contact, and to Bernhard for his thoughtful and careful help. Also to various people who commented on an earlier draft of this paper.

[3] Heine (1976) and Oomen (1977) draw attention to surface forms which are analyzed below as reflexive-middle and have dealt with basic forms of most of the other morphemes I discuss. Sasse (1976) recognizes the reflexive-middle in Rendille.

[4] It is hoped to make available the vocabulary of some 500 verb roots on which the study was based: Sim (1977b).

This paper then attempts to extend the analysis of the Rendille verb by attending to these features. However it remains a brief study with a number of loose ends. In particular the role of prefix extensions is not well elucidated, and their recognition in compounding is incomplete. Also, the problems arising from the juxtaposition of vowels across a morpheme boundary require a lengthier consideration; in general this concerns vowel-initial and vowel-final roots.

2. SYSTEMATIC PHONEMIC SEGMENTS

2.1. Vowels.

There are five contrastive vowel qualities, occurring in two lengths. Unlike Oomen (1977), vowel length is considered phonemic, and long vowels will be written as digraphs.

(1)   *i, ii*   *u, uu*
       e, ee   *o, oo*
                        a, aa

2.2. Consonants.

(2)	labial	apical	palatal	velar	pharyng	glottal
		t	*c*	*k*		
plosives	*b*	*d*	*j*	*g*		
		D				
nasals	*m*	*n*	*ñ*	*ŋ*		
fricatives	*f*	*s*		*x*	*H*	*h*
approximants	*w*	*l, r*	*y*			

D is a retroflexed, post-alveolar plosive, IPA [ɖ], which may be lightly glottalised;
c and *j* are the affricates, IPA [tɕ] and [dʑ] respectively;[5]
H is the pharyngeal fricative, IPA [ħ];
ŋ is known in only three roots: *eyŋasaaw-* 'be surprised', *ŋaay-* 'be surprised', and *ŋur-* 'gash' (possibly the first two of these are derived from the same root).

As will emerge below, consonant gemination is a feature of the language, with a clear role in the verb (its role in other word classes is not discussed).

---

[5] [tɕ] and [dʑ] rather than [tʃ] and [dʒ], although my informant's articulation may be influenced by his attitude towards Swahili, which has [tʃ] and [dʒ]. I assume [ts] and [dz] in Oomen (1978) is a misprint.

2.3. Tone.

Rendille is tonal; little work has been done, however, and in this paper in general only a "prominent-high" is marked for any word.[6]

3. VERB CLASSES

Following Heine (1976) and Oomen (1977), Rendille verbs are divided into two classes: **class 1** consisting of those that inflect by **prefixing**, and **class 2** being those that inflect by **suffixation**. Some thirteen verbs are known to belong to class 1,[7] which will not be considered here. The remainder are class 2 verbs. Full paradigms of verbs will be laid out as follows:

(3)   1st person sing.   1st person plural
              2nd person sing.   2nd person plural
              3rd person sing. masc.   3rd person plural
              3rd person sing. fem.

The scatter of a class 2 root is given in (4). The root *táx-* 'push' is a simple stem chosen for the lack of morphophonemic change it exhibits.

(4)	**affirmative**		**negative**	
imperative	*táx*	*táxa*	*atáxin*	*ataxína*
perfect	*táxe*	*táxne*	*matáxin*	(invariable form)
	táxte	*táxten*		
	táxe	*táxen*		
	táxte			
imperfect	*táxa*	*táxna*	*matáxo*	*matáxno*
	táxta	*táxtan*	*matáxto*	*matáxtan*
	táxa	*táxan*	*matáxo*	*matáxan*
	táxta		*matáxto*	
subjunctive	*táxo*	*táxno*	*itáxin*	(invariable form)
	táxto	*táxtân*[8]		
	táxo	*táxân*		
	táxto			
verbal nouns		*táxnân*		
		táxme		
		taxín		

---

[6]Compare Oomen (1978).

[7]See Oomen (1978). It may also be worth recognizing a set of "hybrid verbs," formed with an adjectival root followed in close-knit sequence by the class 1 verb 'be'. Thus *nucul* 'small' forms *naH a-nucusseHe* 'we are small,' from underlying /nucul-t-eHe/. See Andrzejewski (1969) for hybrid verbs in Somali.

[8]The circumflex denotes a falling tone.

The distinctive basis of the verbal system is displayed by the perfect, the imperfect, and the subjunctive paradigms,[9] and these will be considered first.

4. SIMPLE VERB STEMS

4.1.   The Common Cushitic Pattern and the Suffix Conjugation in Rendille.

The perfect, imperfect and subjunctive aspects exhibit the normal Cushitic "blocking pattern," where person distinctions are introduced in the block element[10] t, n, or ϕ, and aspect depends on the quality of the vowel V.[11] Thus

(5)

	sing.	plural
1st person	-V	-*n*-V
2nd person	-*t*-V	-*t*-V*n*
3rd person masc.	-V	-V*n*
3rd person fem.	-*t*-V	

In the verbal word, this patterning results in a neutralization of (1) 1st person sing. with 3rd person masc. sing. and (2) 2nd person sing. with 3rd person fem. sing.

The specificity of the aspect marker vowel V can be seen below:

(6)

		perfect	imperf.	subjunct.[12]
sing.	1st	-*e*	-*a*	-*o*
	2nd	-*e*	-*a*	-*o*
	3rd masc.	-*e*	-*a*	-*o*
	3rd fem.	-*e*	-*a*	-*o*
plur.	1st	-*e*	-*a*	-*o*
	2nd	-*e(n)*	-*a(n)*	-*a(n)*
	3rd	-*e(n)*	-*a(n)*	-*a(n)*

The structure of the verb in these aspects can be summarized by the formula:

(7)   ROOT + Block Element + Aspect Marker Vowel

---

[9] "Aspect" will be used here simply as a cover term for these paradigms.

[10] Tucker (1967) speaks of the "blocking pattern." What I refer to as the "block element" is explained there as an affix to the root. In the present discussion of class 2 verbs, the element is suffixed to the root:

sing.	1st	ϕ	plur.	1st	n
	2nd	t		2nd	t
	3rd m.	ϕ		3rd	ϕ
	f.	t			

[11] As seen in (4), tone may play a part in aspect determination.

[12] See below, 5.1.5, for qualification of this in the case of reflexive-middle derived stems; also 7.2.3.

Before dealing at length with other forms of the verb, it is convenient to explore the morphophonemic processes operative in the affirmative paradigms of the perfect, imperfect, and subjunctive aspects of simple stem verbs. These processes are basic to an understanding of derived stems (see Section 5 below) and all imperative and negative forms (see Sections 6 and 7 below).

4.2. Morphophonemic Processes.

4.2.1. The Two Consonant Constraint (2 C constraint).

This is perhaps the most basic constraint in the phonology of (East) Cushitic languages: that no clusters of more than two consonants are permitted. A geminated (long) consonant is treated as a two-consonant cluster, and the constraint may be formulated in general terms as

$$(8) \quad * \text{CCC} \quad \text{or} \quad * \begin{bmatrix} C \\ \alpha \text{ gem} \end{bmatrix} \begin{bmatrix} C \\ -\alpha \text{ gem} \end{bmatrix}$$

A natural consequence of this is that (lexical) roots ending in either a cluster of two consonants, or a geminate consonant, introduce an epenthetic vowel to separate the root from a following consonant, e.g. where a block element t or n follows.[13] A morpheme boundary is implicit in potential violations of 2 C constraint and the epenthesis can be handled by a rule of the general form of R 1 operating in a conspiracy with the 2 C constraint.[14]

R 1.   **Epenthesis**   CC + C → CC

The epenthetic vowel is of quality i, although the only examples are given in (9).

(9)	I sent[15]	/éreg-e/[16]	→	érge
	you (sg.) sent	/éreg-t-e/	→	érgite
	we sent	/éreg-n-e/	→	érgine
	I mixed	/wáras-e/	→	wórse[17]
	you (sg.) mixed	/wáras-t-e/	→	wórsite
	we mixed	/wáras-n-e/	→	wórsine

[13] No simple stem verb ending in a geminate consonant is known from among some 500 roots. However, derived stem verbs will be seen later to exhibit the appropriate behaviour. See (28) and (42).

[14] The morphology of other word classes has not been studied but it is clear that many processes are more general and not restricted to the verb. The extent of the generality and the nature of exceptions awaits attention. As a result, categorial restraints are generally not written in this paper.

[15] In fact neither of these roots ends in a cluster in lexical form. Both are subject to the alternation discussed in 4.2.2.1 below, which makes them potential violations of the 2 C restraint. All other roots undergoing this alternation remove violations as in 4.2.2.1.

[16] Slashes / / will denote underlying representations, which are kept as close to surface forms as possible.

[17] A low-level rule converts $a \longrightarrow o$ following w. See also footnote 21.

It can be seen that it is contraction of the root from its lexical form that leads to a configuration prohibited by the 2 C constraint in the derivation; for these two roots this configuration is removed by *i*-epenthesis. A number of other roots show a similar alternation, but potential violations of the constraint are avoided differently. The matter of root alternations and these mechanisms for avoiding violations of the 2 C constraint will be considered now.

4.2.2 Root Alternation and Metathesis.

4.2.2.1. Alternations.

In fact the alternations, which are in some cases accompanied by metathesis,[18] can be understood as an attempt to meet the restrictions imposed by the 2 C constraint. In Rendille these seem to be semi-productive processes, and (10) lists the known examples of class 2 simple stem verbs.[19]

(10)		'I/he'[20]	'you(sg)/she'	'we'
i.	'sleep'	*ŭrde*	*ŭdurte*	*ŭdurre*
ii.	'see'	*årge*	*ågarte*	*ågarre*
iii.	'shiver'	*Hårme*	*Håmarte*	*Håmarre*
iv.	'strike'	*gŭdde*	*gŭdubte*	*gŭdubne*
v.	'be full'	*Dårge*	*Dåragte*	*Dåragne*
vi.	'escape'	*fĭrDe*	*fĭriDDe*	*fĭrinne*
vii.	'share'	*gĭsme*	*gĭsante*	*gĭsanne*
viii.	'be ignorant'	*adalme*	*adalante*	*adalanne*
ix.	'plait'	*jĭrfe*	*jĭrifte*	*jĭrifne*
x.	'knock down'	*asŏ-lŭgde*	*asŏ-lŭgutte*	*asŏ-lŭgunne*
xi.	'feel pain'[21]	*bŏlxe*	*bŏloxte*	*bŏloxne*
xii.	'begin'	*ŭmHe*	*ŭmaHte*	*ŭmaHne*

(iv-xii) involve only alternation; (i-iii) involve both alternation and metathesis. The alternations are summarized in (11).

(11)	**alternation and metathesis**		**alternation only**[22]	
i.	$rd \sim d + V + rt$	iv.	$dd \sim d + V + bt$[23]	
ii.	$rg \sim g + V + rt$	v.	$rg \sim r + V + gt$	
iii.	$rm \sim m + V + rt$	vi.	$rD \sim r + V + D(t)$[24]	

---

[18] Heine (1976) discusses the process of metathesis. While what is said here does not fully explicate the process, it is found to be more widespread and not simply concerned with *r* and *H* as he suggests. Also, I attempt here a phonotactically motivated explanation.

[19] Brief mention is made of derived stem verbs in 5.3.

[20] The form of the root in columns two and three cannot occur in column one. However, the verbal noun form with *-nãn* may occur in two forms, e.g. *årginãn ~ ågarnãn* 'seeing'. See section 8 below.

[21] Heine and Oomen both phonemicise this root as *bolox-*. The first vowel is phonetic [ʊ] and the second phonetic [ɔ].

[22] Display (11) shows forms where the block element is *t*.

[23] *gŭdde ~ gŭdubte* requires some explanation. Sequences of [plosive] [plosive] are few; some of these may be expected to assimilate. I posit here V-deletion without metathesis, followed by assimilation. The derivation is as follows:
$$/g\check{u}dub\text{-}e/ \longrightarrow *gudbe \longrightarrow g\check{u}dde$$

[24] Bracketed consonants ( ) undergo further assimilation.

(11) contd.

alternation only
vii. $sm \sim s + V + (m)t$
viii. $lm \sim l + V + (m)t$
ix. $rf \sim r + V + ft$
x. $gt \sim g + V + tt$
xi. $lx \sim l + V + xt$
xii. $mH \sim m + V + Ht$

An explanation based on the lexical form of the root being the contracted form would require a V-copying process; (vii) and (xii) present difficulty here. More importantly, an explanation of the metathesis is implausible in the light of a comparison of (ii) and (v).

However, if the uncontracted form of the root is taken as the lexical form—the right-hand forms in (11)—then the contraction can be fairly plausibly explained as V-deletion, and the metathesis also is capable of a phonotactic explanation (see below, 4.2.2.2).

The restraints placed on the V-deletion by the environment are noteworthy. First, generally (but not invariably), the vowel to be deleted must be of the same quality as the vowel in the preceding syllable. A corollary of this is that the process can only occur with roots of at least two syllables.

Secondly, the two consonants which cluster must both be ungeminated, and the second of these must not be followed by either a consonant or a word boundary. These restrictions are imposed by the 2 C constraint.

R $2'$ accomplishes the V-deletion by incorporating this degree of constraint.

$$R\,2'. \qquad \textbf{V-deletion} \qquad V_i \;\rightarrow\; \phi \;\Big/\; V_i \begin{bmatrix} C_1 \\ \text{-gem} \end{bmatrix}\!\!-\!\!\begin{bmatrix} C_2 \\ \text{-gem} \end{bmatrix}\!\! + \; V$$
$$\text{ROOT}$$

However, this fails to make explicit the role of the 2 C constraint and perhaps the better formalization would be to set up a rule R 2 operating in conspiracy with the 2 C constraint.

$$R\,2. \qquad \textbf{V-deletion} \qquad V_i \;\rightarrow\; \phi \;\Big/\; V_i C\underline{\hspace{2cm}}C+$$

Two counter-examples to the restriction on vowel quality are (vii) and (xii).

A number of roots are known which do not undergo this V-deletion and which suggest that R 2 must be further restricted to exclude deletion of a long vowel, to exclude formation of a geminate consonant,[25] to exclude roots derived by prefix extensions (below 5.4), and to exclude contraction of any monosyllabic root having the reduplicative (below 5.5).

---

[25] This must be qualified: some roots do not contract even when this would be predicted by the explanation given. Also it should be noted that there is one counterexample to this avoidance: the forms *gollice* and *gololice* 'I fed' (causative) are both known.

4.2.2.2. Metathesis.

The relevant examples from (10) are repeated below.

(12)   'I slept'   /údur-e/   →   *udre   →   ůrde
       'I saw'   /ágar-a/   →   *agre   →   árge
       'I shivered'   /Hámar-e/   →   *Hamre   →   Hårme

The metathesis is suggested as an attempt to remove non-permissible clusters which have been formed by the previous V-deletion process contracting the root. This can be supported by several pieces of evidence.

First, it affords a rationalization of the surface forms of *ågar- ~ árg-* 'see' and *Dårag- ~ Dårg-* 'be full'. That is, a contracted form *ågr-* contains a non-permissible cluster, and this is removed by metathesis.

Secondly, an examination of permissible clusters in Rendille suggests certain non-permissible sequences. The schema in (13) summarizes the known clustering possibilities within the morpheme.[26]

(13)
C_1	C_2: plos.	fric.	nasal.	post-alv.	approxim.
approxim.	x	x	x(n)	x	x
nasal	x	x(h)		x(h)	
laryng. H,h	x	x(s)	x(m)		
plosive	x	x(s)			
fric.	x(s)	x(s)			

Attested clusters are marked by "x". The parenthesized segments (n), (m), (s) indicate that such sequences are only known with these segments as one member. The indication (h) indicates that only homorganic sequences are known in these cases. The sequence [fricative] [fricative] is only known with s as second member.

While no rigorous generalization can be made, there seems to be a real basis for positing certain sequences to be non-permissible. Two examples will demonstrate the application of this. Perhaps the clearest case concerns the non-permissibility of *[non-approximant] [approximant]. This excludes such clusters as undergo metathesis in (12) above. Thus: *gr, *dr, *mr, and this can be extended by the data in (14) below.

(14)   'bag'   ugår ;   plural: urgő   *ugro
          'clothing' dafår ;   plural: darfő   *dafro
          'eat!'   áHam ;   plural: atåmHin   *ataHmin

Thus a constraint *[non-approximant] [approximant] can be posited and any violation of this resulting from application of R 2 is entry to a metathesis rule.

---

[26] Known clusters include: *lb, ld, lj, lD, lm, lf, lx, lH, lw, ly, rb, rd, rg, rt, rk, rD, rm, rn, rf, rs, rx, rH, rl, ws, yn, Hb, Ht, Hs, xs, sk, sm, fl, ŋg, ŋk, gx, nj, nd, nt, nD, ns, mb, mH, bd, bg, bs, bH, gd, gt, ks.* Some gaps can be filled by reference to the assimilation processes discussed in this paper, and other gaps may be filled by a larger corpus. It is felt at this stage that a formalization in terms of distinctive features would be premature. The known clusters are taken from Heine (1976) and Sim (1977b).

Secondly, the cluster *[fricative] [nasal] is unknown and expected to be non-permissible; [nasal] [fricative] clusters are limited to the homorganic sequences *ns* and *ŋx*. It seems reasonable to predict sequences *mx/xm* and *nx/xn* to be non-permissible also.[27] This affords an explanation of the data in (15).

(15)	'neck'	*luxúm* ;	plural:	*luxumó*	**luxmó*	(cf. Konso: *xolm-*)
					*lumxó	
	'sinew'	*buxún* ;	plural	*buxunó*	**buxnó*	
					*bunxó	

Now, if clusters **mx, *xm, *nx, *xn* are non-permissible, a metathesis rule cannot resolve non-permissible forms which would be introduced by the V-deletion rule discussed already. In cases such as (15) then, entry to the V-deletion rule R 2 is excluded on the grounds that the metathesis rule which follows, cannot remove the non-permissible forms. Here is an interesting case of a "peeking rule" in the sense of Hill (1970), where a "peek" at the output of the metathesis rule determines entry to the previous rule R 2.

Finally, all other known cases of contraction conform to the formation of known, permissible clusters, without resorting to metathesis. Thus:

(16)	'ram'	*Helèm*	plurals:	*Helmó*
	'tear(n.)'	*ilim*		*ilmó*
	'shoulder blade'	*gårab*		*garbó*
	'ear'	*nabåH*		*nabHó*
	'charcoal'	*jiláH*		*jilHó*

In conclusion then, a second basic constraint should be formulated within the phonology of Rendille, one that formalizes the permissible consonant clusters and thereby defines the non-permissible clusters. A metathesis rule must then be in conspiracy with this constraint so that it operates only in cases of violation of this restriction on permitted sequences. R 3 provides a simple formulation of such a rule, which, under the conspiracy provided by the permissible clusters constraint, will only apply in cases of violation, and will not re-apply if the first application resolves the violation.

R 3   **Metathesis** $C_1 C_2 \rightarrow C_2 C_1$

Indeed, R 2 and R 3 must both enter into this conspiracy, so that if a first application of R 3 does not remove a violation, then neither R 2 nor R 3 is to be applied to the derivation of forms. R 2 then may operate only where (a) its output does not violate the permissibility constraint or (b) any violations are removed by R 3. In other words, the output of R 3 acts as a phonotactic constraint upon the input to R 2.

---

[27] I am considering morpheme internal clusters here. The restriction to homorganic sequences does not apply across a morpheme boundary. The exclusion of *nx/xn* implies that the adjustment of phonemic *nx* to phonetic [ŋx] is disallowed. This constraint may be formalized as

$$*\begin{bmatrix} +nas \\ \alpha\ grave \\ \beta\ ant \end{bmatrix} \begin{bmatrix} +cont \\ +voice \\ -\alpha\ grave \\ -\beta\ ant \end{bmatrix}$$

That is, the possibility of the two segments in a [nasal] [fricative] cluster differing in their values of grave and anterior is disallowed.

4.2.3. Assimilations Due to the Block Element.

There are a number of assimilatory processes resulting from the introduction of the block element *t* or *n*, which will be considered in turn. (Note that these apply only to the block element (cf. the verbal noun form -*nân*, in Section 7 below).

4.2.3.1. *t*-Assmiliations.

This includes the forms 2nd person singular and plural and 3rd person feminine singular.

(a) The apicals and palatals *t*,[28] *d*, *s*, *j*, and *D* assimilate the block element completely to themselves. No root is known ending in *c*. (Compare 5.3 for a different assimilation with **stem**-final *c*).
   Relevant data includes that in (17).

(17)	'you pulled'	/jíit-t-e/	→	jíitte[29]
	'you shaved'	/Háad-t-e/	→	Háadde[29]
	'you rested'	/nás-t-e/	→	násse
	'you tried'	/káj-t-e/	→	kájje
	'you tied'	/HíD-t-e/	→	HíDDe
	'you passed the day'	/HáD-t-e/	→	HáDDe

The following rule achieves this.

R 4.   *t*-**assimilation**
$$\left. \begin{matrix} t \\ d \\ s \\ j \\ D \end{matrix} \right\} + \quad t \quad \rightarrow \quad \left\{ \begin{matrix} tt \\ dd \\ ss \\ jj \\ DD \end{matrix} \right.$$

A feature specification $\begin{bmatrix} \text{- vocalic} \\ \text{+coronal} \\ \text{- nasal} \end{bmatrix}$ would be useful here, apart from the case of root-final *c*, about which nothing is known.

(b) The lateral *l* followed by *t*.[30]

(18)	'you will give birth'	/Dél-t-a/	→	Déssa
	'you will decorate'	/kúlkul-t-a/	→	kúlkússa
	'you will carve'	/yéel-t-a/	→	yéessa

---

[28] *t* is included in order to recognize the generality of the process.

[29] There is a general phonetic rule reducing long vowels to semi-long before CC, C-gem, or C# .

[30] This process is operative in noun morphology also: /maxabál-ti/ → *maxabássi* 'the woman who ...'. Oomen offers one exception (personal communication): *ricultisa* 'his smallness'. *ricul* and *nucul* seem to be freely variant forms, in which case it is worth noting that the exception does not extend to the hybrid-verb form /a-nucul-t-eHe/ → *a-nucusseHe* 'you are small'.

R 5.   *lt*-assimilation $l + t \rightarrow ss$[31]

(c) Root-final nasals assimilate to the block element in point of articulation, although no roots are known ending in *ñ* or *ŋ*.[32]

(19)	'you ground'	/túm-t-e/	→	*tŭnte*
	'you got wet'	/xúyyam-t-e/	→	*xŭyyante*
	'you played'	/girdám-t-e/	→	*girdânte*

R 6.   **nasal-assimilation** $m \ + \ t \ \rightarrow \ nt$

4.2.3.2.   *n*-Assimilations.

This refers to first person plural forms.

(a) Root-final *t* and *D* assimilate completely to following *n*. It is necessary to consider a variety of data here.

(20)	(i)	'we stole'	/Hát-n-e/	→	*Hánne*
		'we dug'	/xót-n-e/	→	*xónne*
		'we paid'	/kút-n-e/	→	*kŭnne*
		'we won'	/gút-n-e/	→	*gŭnne*
		'we pulled'	/jíit-n-e/	→	*jírinne*
	(ii)	'we tied'	/HíD-n-e/	→	*Híinne*
		'we passed the day'	/HáD-n-e/	→	*Háanne*
	(iii)	'we spoke'	/yéeD-n-e/	→	*yéenne*
		'we were happy'	/HamáaD-n-e/	→	*Hamáanne*
		'we escaped'	/fíriD-n-e/	→	*fírinne*

A straightforward rule such as R 7 is required.

R 7. $\begin{Bmatrix} t \\ D \end{Bmatrix} \ + \ n \ \longrightarrow \ nn$

However from the data in (20)(ii) it is clear that a V-lengthening rule[33] is operative also, for roots ending in *D*. This seems to be restricted to CVC roots, and poses problems as to the exact form and order of the necessary rules. However, a compensatory V-lengthening rule R 8 can be roughly formulated, and ordered to precede R 7.

---

[31] R. Hetzron has drawn my attention to the situation in Somali, where $l + t \rightarrow š$, and suggests the changes $lt \rightarrow l \rightarrow$ *š* as one phonetically plausible explanation here.

[32] Any nasal becomes homorganic with a following consonant across a morpheme boundary. Within the morpheme only homorganic sequences occur. A feature notation rule readily captures this generality. The loan *soom*- 'read' from Swahili *soma* 'read!' also assimilates. See note 34 below.

[33] A similar situation exists in Konso, where assimilation of Konso implosives with a following block element involves compensatory vowel lengthening also. See Sim (1977a). Rendille *D* and the implosive *D* in Konso are reflexes of the same Proto East Cushitic segment.

R 8.   V   →   [+ long] $\Big/$ $\begin{bmatrix} C \underline{\hspace{1em}} / D / \\ R \qquad\quad R \end{bmatrix}$ +   n

An alternative solution would be to set up a conspiracy such that monosyllabic *D*-final roots which are input to R 7 are obligatory input also to R 8, (which then may be substantially simplified to V → [+ long]), but only those roots are input to R 8.

Note that the other coronals discussed in 4.2.3.1 (a), i.e. *s*, *d*, and *j*, do not undergo n-assimilation.

(21)   'we rested'   *nåsne*
              'we tried'   *kåjne*
              'we shaved'   *Håadne*

(b)   *l* and *r* assimilate following *n* completely to themselves; with *r* it is an optional rule.

(22)   'we gave birth'   /Dél-n-e/   →   *Dĕlle*
              'we carved'   /yéel-n-e/   →   *yĕelle*
              'we opened'   /fůr-n-e/   →   *fůrre ~ fůrne*
              'we saw'   /ågar-n-e/   →   *ågarre ~ ågarne*

R 9. $\begin{Bmatrix} l \\ r \end{Bmatrix}$ +   *n*   → $\begin{Bmatrix} ll \\ rr \end{Bmatrix}$

(c)   Root-final nasals assimilate completely to following *n*.[34],[35]

(23)   'we ground'   /tům-n-e/   →   *tůnne*
              'we aimed'   /bim-n-e/   →   *bînne*
              'we ran off'   /ñáam-n-e/   →   *nåanne*

R 10.   *m*   +   *n*   →   *nn*

From the scatter given in (4) for the root *tåx-* 'push', it can be seen that two forms of the verbal noun −*tåxnån*, *tåxme*−introduce a similar phonological environment to that in R 7-10. However, no assimilation takes place in the verbal noun forms with root-final *l*. *D* and *m* do assimilate, and *r* may optionally.[36]

---

[34] Rendille *soom-* 'read' and *chora* 'write' are borrowed from the Swahili forms *soma* and *chora* with the same meanings. These loans undergo the morphemic changes discussed in rules M 6, 9, 10, suggesting that these rules are percepts of the native speaker.   .

[35] Root final *ñ* and *ŋ* have not been found.

[36] Consonants may be ranked according to the assimilation processes to which they are subject.

5. DERIVED STEM VERBS

Here the reflexive-middle and causative stems are dealt with, i.e. the suffix extension elements which immediately follow the verb root.[37],[38] The prefix extensions are mentioned next, and finally the reduplicative.

5.1. The Reflexive-Middle.[39]

Heine (1976) avoids recognizing a reflexive-middle morpheme, although he presents relevant data, suggesting that such verbs be treated as a sub-group. Oomen (1977) and (1978) develops this into her Class 2 B verbs, which she further subdivides into 2 Ba and 2 Bb, on the basis that the latter subgroup displays a surface form ending in *-so* in the imperative singular.[40]

It is preferable to recognize a separate morpheme, whose role is broadly that of **benefactive** or **reflexive-middle**, and since the morpheme is semi-productive (as is the causative) all sub-classifications of Class 2 verbs can be dispensed with. Roots that are obligatorily reflexive-middle (or obligatorily causative) are a matter for the lexicon. In short then, when the productive nature of the morpheme and the derived stem nature of such verbs are recognized, there is no need to subdivide Class 2. Such derived stems introduce regularities which can be readily explained by rule. The occurrence of the element *-s-* in some stems, with the reflexive-middle is discussed in 5.2 below.

Hayward (1975) indicates four functions of the reflexive-middle morpheme[41] in ᶜAfar, Oromo, and Somali, which are discernible in Rendille also.

5.1.1. Autobenefactive Use.

This, the middle voice proper,

> "indicates that the subject of the clause performs the action or participates in the event denoted by the verb expressly for his own benefit."   (Hayward 1975:209).

---

[37]These two apparently cannot co-occur, although either can occur with the simple reflexive prefix extension *is-*. Thus *isxåbte* 'it became solid' (= 'it caught itself') derives from /is-xâb-âD-e/, and *isDågce* 'he ambushed' derives from /is-Dág-îc-e/.

[38]The terms "reflexive-middle" and below "auto-benefactive" are taken over from Hayward (1975).

[39]"Reflexive-middle" seems to be the most appropriate cover term, since it subsumes "benefactive," a term which, alone, is rather too specific for application to some derived stems. For Galab (Dasenech), Sasse (1976) has used the term "subjective" for a similar form.

[40]It is the *s* that is distinctive for her: the final vowel occurs in all her class 2 B verbs in imperative singular. See below, Section 6. At best this is an insufficient criterion, since it fails to distinguish s-final roots from Class 2 B.

[41]The fourth of these, comprising denominal and deadjectival stems he considers as incorporating a verbalizing affix of identical shape to that of the reflexive-middle. However, he later suggests that this inchoativizing role arose out of an extension of the role of the reflexive-middle. He is able in ᶜAfar to distinguish two formatives on formal grounds. This is not yet possible in Rendille, although the matter has bearing in any treatment of what I have already referred to as "hybrid verbs."

In Rendille a number of stems clearly have this connotation, as is seen in the wide range of concepts in (24).[42]

(24)	'marry' (=build house for self)	DísD-
	'kiss'	DongáD-
	'rape'	lagdåD-
	'boast' (=describe self for own benefit)	is-cêegD-
	'send for'	ergáD-
	'hunt'	eysåD-
	'cheat'	ekkêsD-
	'burn for self'	gûbD-

While in some cases the auto-benefactive sense is idiosyncratic, e.g. 'marry', and in others the simple stem is not used (*Dong-), this function is otherwise productive. Simple stems such as *gub-* 'burn', *gat-* 'buy', *jiit-* 'pull', *xot-* 'dig' can also take the reflexive middle morpheme with a clearly auto-benefactive addition to their meaning.

5.1.2. Reflexive Use.

This

> "indicates that the subject necessarily performs the action denoted by the verb upon himself, or that he performs some action which usually requires volition on his part and only ever involves his own person."   (Hayward 1975:211).

Epistemic verbs and many verbs of body function or response belong here.

(25)	'bathe' (=wash self)	DíxD-
	'warm self'	DaHamóoD-
	'smile'	mûsD-
	'breathe'	nebsåD-
	'learn'	åbD-
	'believe'	rumêesD- ~ rumeysåD-
	'decorate self'	kulkûlD-
	'comb' (own hair)	fílD-

5.1.3. Idiosyncratic Use.

The verbs listed here tend to be intransitive (the event carried out by or upon the grammatical subject). Often there is no simple stem, or the derived stem meaning is idiosyncratic in comparison.

---

[42] These stems are cited in the surface forms of the 1st person singular. *D* or *aD* is the reflexive-middle morpheme.

(26)   'catch'   *xåbD-*
              'throw spear'   *tarbåD-*
              'go'   *írD-*
              'go back'   *nóxD-*
              'go near'   *sooDowåaD-*
              'be finished' (=dying)   *massåD-*

5.1.4. Denominal/Deadjectival Use.

The central idea seems to be that of "being or becoming a certain state". While on the one hand the
clear verbalizing role tempts one to think in terms of a second morpheme homophonous with the reflexive-
middle, there is a close connection semantically with a reflexive: 'becoming thin' is close to 'thinning
oneself' (the first is presumably involuntary). Lack of formal grounds for separating this function leads
one to consider it as an extension of the role of the reflexive-middle.[43]

(27)   'be ill'   *xannåD-*   cf.   'illness':   *xanaat*
          'be thin'   *roxxåD-*   cf.   'thin':   *roxxan*
          'become green'   *ulHåaD-*   cf.   'green':   *uleH*

As suggested above, there is a blurring of functions, and it is not always simple to decide to which
of these four any one stem belongs.

5.1.5. The Form of the Reflexive-Middle.

The following paradigms of the perfect aspect make clear the variety of surface forms.

(28)	*xab-*[44]	*xann-*	*amans-*[45]	*HalalDu-*	: Roots
	'catch'	'be ill'	'yawn'	'chew'	: derived stem gloss
1st sg.	*xåbDe*	*xannåDe*	*amansåDe*	*HalalDúuDe*	
2nd	*xåbatte*	*xannåtte*	*amansåtte*	*HalalDúutte*	
3rd m.	*xåbte*	*xannåte*	*amansåte*	*HalalDúute*	
3rd f.	*xåbatte*[46]	*xannåtte*	*amansåtte*	*HalalDúutte*	
1st pl.	*xåbanne*	*xannånne*	*amansånne*	*HalalDúunne*	
2nd pl.	*xåbatten*	*xannåtten*	*amansåtten*	*HalalDúutten*	
3rd pl.	*xåbten*	*xannåten*	*amansåten*	*HalalDúuten*	

(a) Much generality can be abstracted by setting up an underlying representation *åD* for the formative.[47]
The display (29) below summarizes much of the generality underlying the divergent surface forms.

---

[43] Note that in hybrid verbs, the morpheme is frequently dropped from perfect aspect forms.

[44] Cp. Konso *xapt-* 'throw'.

[45] Note the *s*. See 5.2 below.

[46] Heine (1976) records a vowel *e* in 3rd person feminine singular forms. This may be a matter of dialect.

[47] This is the form set up for Konso (Sim 1977a), where it more often approximates to the surface form. Cp. Hayward's
recognition of a "vowel-*D/t*" shape (Hayward 1975). His arguments seem preferable to those of Bliese (1973).

(29)   Following root-final $\left\{ \begin{array}{l} \text{CC} \\ \text{C-gem} \end{array} \right\}$ the surface form is $\mathring{a}D$

$\qquad\qquad\qquad\qquad\qquad$ C $\qquad\qquad$ the surface form is D

$\qquad\qquad\qquad\qquad\qquad$ V $\qquad\qquad$ the surface form is $\acute{V}D$

Thus, the 2 C rule is operative, and is the major generalization not recognized by Heine or Oomen. Where the root ends in an ungeminated consonant, there is vowel deletion and clustering of consonants. This is developed below, in the remainder of this section.

(b) A distinction is created[48] between 1st person singular and 3rd person masculine singular. This only occurs in Rendille with reflexive-middle stems. A rule such as R 11 is required.

R 11.

$$D \quad \rightarrow \quad t \quad / \quad \left[\begin{array}{c} \underline{\qquad} \\ <\text{REF-MID}> \\ <\text{3rd PERS}> \\ <\text{MASC/PL}> \end{array} \right]$$

As noted in R 11, the reflexive-middle surfaces with a *t* in 3rd person plural forms also.

(c) The aspect vowel in the subjunctive forms is characteristically *i* rather than *o* as elsewhere (see Section 3 above, data block (4)), in reflexive-middle stems. Note that the same alternation is true also of the negative imperfect forms (7.2.3 below).

(d) The surfacing of a vowel *a* in forms of the reflexive-middle is subject to the restriction imposed by the 2 C constraint. First, in any environment with a following block element *t* or *n* or where the root terminates in a consonant cluster or geminate consonant, the vowel cannot be deleted. The schema in (30) summarizes these environments:

(30)   C + ___ C + C   (a following block element)

$\qquad\quad$ CC + ___ C +   (a preceding cluster)

Secondly, only in the environment of (31) can the vowel be deleted.

(31)   VC + ___ C + V

If the influence of the 2 C constraint in the phonology of Rendille is recognized as forming a basic constraint, then again the postulation of a V-deletion rule R 12 in conspiracy with the 2 C constraint derives the correct surface forms. The environmental restriction in (31) is a consequence of the 2 C constraint, and need not be explicitly stated in R 12.

R 12   V $\rightarrow \phi$ $/ \quad \left[\begin{array}{c} \underline{\qquad} \text{C} \\ <\text{EXT}_s> \end{array} \right]$

$<\text{EXT}_s>$ restricts the deletion to the case of suffix extensions. (In 5.3 below R 12 will be seen to apply also to causative stems).

---

[48]This also occurs in 1st person and 3rd person masc. singular forms in ^CAfar; see also Hayward (1975) and Bliese (1973).

(e) In cases where this deletion cannot apply, the reflexive-middle *D* assimilates completely to a following block element according to the *t*- and *n*- assimilation rules R 4 and R 7 respectively.

Where the vowel of the reflexive-middle is deleted, a consonant cluster is formed with the root-final consonant.

(32)	'I caught'	/ xab-aDe /	→ *xabDe*
	'I was born'	/ Del-aD-e /	→ *DelDe*
	'I went'	/ ir-aD-e /	→ *irDe*
	'I married (=built myself a house)'	/ Dis-aD-e /	→ *DisDe*

(f) Certain assimilations may take place in this surface cluster. First, in 3rd person masculine and plural forms, where *D* surfaces as *t* according to R 11, the normal *t*-assimilation rules then apply.

(33)	'they shaved'	/ Haad-aD-en /	→ / HaadDen /	→ / Haadten /	→ *Haatten*
	'he stalked'	/ kol-aD-e /	→ / kolDe /	→ / kolte /	→ *kosse*
	'he sat down'	/ orrom-aD-e /	→ / orromDe /	→ / orromte /	→ *orronte*

In forms where R 11 does not apply, i.e. for 1st person sg., a root-extension assimilation is operative for roots ending in *t* and *d* (*D* can be included for completeness).

(34)	'I shaved'	/ Haad-aD-e /	→ / HaadDe /	→ *HaaDDe*
	'I pulled for myself'	/ jiit-aD-e -/	→ / jiitDe /	→ *jiiDDe*
	'I revenged myself'	/ mog (a)gud-aD-a /	→ / mog gudDe /	→ *mog guDDe*
	'I sat down'	/ orrom-aD-e /	→ / orromDe /	→ *orronDe*

(In both (33) and (34) note that the root final nasal assimilates to the following consonant in point of articulation.) This root/extension assimilation requires rule R 13:

R 13.
$$\begin{Bmatrix} t \\ d \\ D \end{Bmatrix} + D_e \quad \rightarrow \quad DD$$

(g) There is assimilation, in vowel-final roots, of the vowel in the reflexive-middle to the root-final vowel, with formation of a long vowel. This **vowel assimilation** rule is formulated as R 14:

R 14. $V \quad \rightarrow \quad V' \; / \; V' + \underline{\quad}$

(h) Finally, an examination of the data in (28) reveals that tone also plays a surface role in reflexive-middle forms. Various explanatory derivations could be compared, but at present it will only be noted that stems whose roots end in a single consonant (ungeminated) bear a prominent high tone on the root. In other stems, the prominent high appears on the vocalic segment of the reflexive-middle formative.

R 15. $(\acute{\;}) . . C C (_{E\acute{X}T}) \quad \rightarrow \quad (\;\;) . . C C (_{E\acute{X}T})$

5.2. The Affix *s* with Reflexive-Middle Stems.

The recognition of a morpheme of this shape and the nature of its role is difficult for several reasons. Only in fifteen stems with the reflexive-middle is this latter preceded by an *s* element. No case has been recognized of its occurrence in the absence of the reflexive-middle.

In only four of the known examples does a clear-cut, readily related simple stem occur for comparison:[49]

(35)	'stand up'	/ tólol-s-áD- /	→	tolossâD-	cf.	tolol-	'stand'
	'eat'	/ gólol-s-áD- /	→	golossâD-		golol-	'eat'
						(golol,	'food')
	'keep for oneself'	/ gíl-s-áD- /	→	gissâD-		gil-	'put in'
	'intend, plan for self'	/ tól-s-áD- /	→	tossâD-		tol	'plan' (noun)

In two other cases it is more difficult to derive the surface form of the verb from known cognates which do not have a segment *s*.

(36)	'I believed'	rumêesDe	cp.	rum	'truth'
	'I praised'	kalanéesDe		kalât	'praise' (N)

There is some plausibility in the derivation of at least the first of these from a causative:[50]

(37)	'truth' (N)	rum	
	'make true (V)	rum-(ee)s	(causative)
	'make true for oneself'	rumeesD-	
	(=believe)		

In seven cases, a cognate noun also exhibits an *s*:

(38)		**Verb**	**Noun**
	'breath'	nebsâD-	nebsi
	'blink'	dumunsâD-	dumunsi
	'yawn'	amansâD-	amansi
	'number/count'	ekkaysâD-	ekkaas
	'spit'	bidixsâD-	bidixsi
	'hunt'	eysâD-	eysi
	'prayer/pray'	weysâD-[51] ~ wêesD-	weysi

For at least *nebs-* 'breath', the proto-Afroasiatic root *n-p-š-* suggests that the *s* be here recognized as belonging to the root. In the others, the weight of evidence is in this direction also.

In the two remaining cases, no cognate forms have been recognized:

(39)	'wear'	gessâD-	
	'pay attention'	DagansáD-	(but cf. 'hear' Dag-)

---

[49] Note that all these roots end in *l*. The assimilation is l + s → ss.

[50] This is the derivation in Boran, from a non-cognate: / Duga-is-ad- / → *DugeefaD-* 'believe'.

[51] These two forms are discussed in note 58.

The clearest data is in (35) above. The following display (40) shows a little more clearly the relationship between simple and derived stems for these examples.

(40)	**simple stems**		**derived stems**	
	'put in'	*gil-*	'put in/keep for oneself'	*gil-s-åD-*
	'feed'	*golol-*	'feed oneself' (=eat)	*golol-s-åD-*
	'stand'	*tolol-*	'stand up' (oneself)	*tolol-s-åD-*
	'plan' (noun)	*tol*	'plan for self'	*tol-s-åD-*

This is slight evidence on which to conclude that the role of *s* is to introduce another agentive,[52] but it is not implausible. Thus:

(41)   *gil-*   'put in' requires one agent: 'someone put in . .'

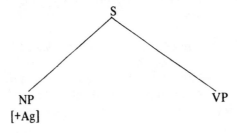

       gissaD-   'put in for oneself' requires two agents, although they have a single referent:

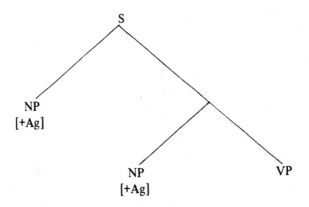

---

[52] See Hayward's treatment of this.

This treatment incidentally suggests a reason for the co-occurrence of *s* with a subset of reflexive-middle stems: *s* is required in those reflexive-middle stems whose simple stems would not normally require more than one agentive noun phrase. Since the function of the causative may be taken as introducing an agentive,[53] *s* forms are not expected in that construction.

5.3. The Causative.

The following paradigms make clear the major surface forms to be accounted for.

(42)		*kar-*	*xorx-*	*goll-*	*goo-*	: Root
		'cook'	'swallow'	'feed'	'cut'	: derived stem meaning
	1st sg.	*kárce*	*xorxíce*	*gollíce*	*góoce*	
	2nd	*kárisse*	*xorxísse*	*gollísse*	*góosse*	
	3rd m.	*kárce*	*xorxíce.*	*gollíce.*	*góoce*	
	3rd f.	*kárisse*	*xorxísse*	*gollísse*	*góosse*	
	1st pl.	*kárinne*	*xorxínne*	*gollínne*	*góonne*	
	2nd	*kárissen*	*xorxíssen*	*gollíssen*	*góossen*	
	3rd	*kárcen*	*xorxícen*	*gollícen*	*góocen*	

(a) Setting up an underlying form *íc* allows statement of many generalizations. The usual neutralization of 1st person singular with 3rd person masculine is maintained. Otherwise generalizations similar to those that were made above (5.1.5) for the reflexive-middle are applicable here also:

(43)	Following		
	monosyllabic CVC	the surface form is *c*	
	⎧ polysyllabic roots ⎫		
	⎨ root-final -CC ⎬	the surface form is *ic*	
	⎩ -VVC ⎭		
	root-final V	the surface form is V*c* ~ *yc*	

The difference between this and the corresponding summary (29) for the reflexive-middle, lies in the closer constraints placed on roots whose final consonant clusters with the causative *c*. Thus, of consonant-final roots, only those that are monosyllabic and whose vowel is short, undergo vowel deletion and consequent clustering of the causative *c* with the root final consonant.[54] The Vowel Deletion Rule, R 12, in 5.1.5 (d) must then be subject to this additional constraint.

The data in (44) illustrates this constraint on vowel deletion.

(44)	'I herded'	*yuubíce.*
	'I grazed (tr.)'	*yaaxíce.*
	'I dried (tr.)'	*angagíce*
	'I greeted'	*baridíce.*

---

[53] It seems likely that *s* is a causative morpheme. See Boran, for instance, where 1st cycle causatives pattern in a similar way.

[54] An alternative analysis would be to set up *c* as the underlying form of the causative, in which case surface forms are derived by i-epenthesis rather than V-deletion, in the second set of environments listed in (43). In deriving a form such as *karisse*, 'you cooked' from / kar-c-te / the epenthetic vowel can be correctly inserted if epenthesis operates from the the root outwards. However it is difficult in this analysis to account satisfactorily for the alternations in the 1st person forms recorded in (49), and summarized in (43) for root final vowels.

(b) Assimilations of the causative *c* with the block element (see data in (42) above) require the formulation of two further rules.

R 16.   *c* + *t*   →   *ss*

R 17.   *c* + *n*   →   *nn*

As with the reflexive-middle, assimilation with the block element is ordered to precede V-deletion and clustering with root-final consonants in roots of the shape (C)VC.

(c) Assimilation of the root-final consonant with the causative *c* is known in the cases in (45). Note that these are all monosyllabic roots with a short vowel, i.e. they are input to the Vowel Deletion Rule R 12.

(45)

	fit-	*jit-*	*sid-*	*gil-*	*Hol-*	*xom-*
	'make straight'	'extinguish'	'carry'	'put in'	'bargain'	'make straight'
1st/3rd m.	*fîcce*[55]	*jîcce*[55]	*sîcce*[55]	*gîsse*	*Hôsse*	*xônce*
2nd/3rd f.	*fîtisse*	*jîtisse*	*sîdisse*	*gîlisse*	*Hôlisse*	*xômisse*
1st pl.	*fîtinne*	*jîtinne*	*sîdinne*	*gîlinne*	*Hôlinne*	*xôminne*
3rd pl.	*fîccen*	*jîccen*	*sîccen*	*gîssen*	*Hôssen*	*xôncen*

Root-final *l* is known on some occasions not to assimilate, in violation of the regularity postulated in (45):

(46)   'I caused (him) to remember'   *kasoelce*
        'I caused (him) to sew it'   *tolce*[56]
        'I caused (him) to skin it'   *xalce*[56]

If the assimilated forms in (45) are taken as the normal case, rule R 18 can be formalized:

R 18.   *t* + *c*   →   *cc*

Assimilation with root-final *D* seems to be avoided: *HiD-* 'tie' is the only monosyllabic root noted and the form *aHiDice* is the form suggested by the informant.[57] The only other case noted is with root *firiD-* 'escape', where only the contracted form of the root appears on the surface. Thus

(47)   'I made (him) escape'   *fîrDice*
        'you made (him) escape'   *fîrDisse*
        'we made (him) escape'   *fîrDinne*

---

[55] The point here is that no phonetic transcription would allow recovery of the root-final consonant. The argument does not rest on the accuracy of the phonemicized transcription adopted here.

[56] The forms *tolce* and *xalce* are not in regular use. Constructions such as ' "skin it!" I told him' are preferred.

[57] The form *a-* is a focus marker. This form is not in use apparently; again the construction noted in footnote 56 is preferred.

This extends the treatment in 4.2.2.1 above. Here in (47) the underlying stem is *firiD-îc-*, which provides the environment necessary for the Root Contraction R 2 to occur. This rule then can be ordered to precede the Vowel Deletion Rule R 12. The ordering of t- and n-Assimilation Rules is unaffected. Here again the pervasiveness of the 2 C constraint in the phonology of Rendille is apparent.

Root-final *s* and *r* do not assimilate:

(48)   'I made (him) rest (=I took his load)'   *nåsce*
        'I cooked'   *kårce*

(d) Causative stems derived from vowel-final roots surface in a variety of forms.

(49)

	1st person	**2nd person**
'recounted (tale)'	*Hawôyce ~ Hawôoce*	*Hawôosse*
'swallowed'	*xorxêyce ~ xorxîice*	*xorxî(i)sse*
'spoiled'	*suujåyce ~ suujåace*	*suujåasse*
'loosened'	*futennåyce ~ futennåace*	*futennåasse*
'renewed'	*Husubnåyce ~ ?*	*Husubnåasse*

Two general processes are operative. First, there may be complete assimilation of the vowel of the causative to the final vowel of the root, with formation of a single long vowel. This is covered by R 14, set up for the same assimilation in reflexive-middle stems. Secondly, the vowel of the causative may diphthongize following a root-final vowel.

R 19.   *ic*   →   *yc*   /   V   +   ___

As can be seen from (49), the resultant forms are generally in variation where there is no block element.[58] The root *goo-* 'cut' assimilates obligatorily (see (42)). One root undergoes neither process: *Daî-* 'fry'.

(50)   'I fried'   *Daîce*
        'you fried'   *Daîsse*

In both cases the root-final vowel has a value of two moras.
In forms with a block element *t* or *n*, assimilation rather than dipthongization is operative.

5.4. Prefix Extensions.

Only a few notes relevant to morphophonemic alternation will be made here. The recognition of an element as a verbal extension prefixing the root has been restricted to those elements that are themselves prefixed by the negative prefix (in negative forms! See 7.1). They are *sô-* ~ 'towards the speaker', *is-* reflexive, *ka-* ablative/instrumental, *le-* 'with', the latter two being pre-verbal case-markers.

---

[58] By stating the dipthongization rule in the approximate form i   → *y* / V ___ and ordering it to precede the vowel deletion rule R 12 (section 5.1.5 (d)) which contracts the reflexive-middle, it is possible to account for such forms as *weysåDa* 'pray!' (plural) /we-is-aD-a/. If the dipthongization rule is also in disjunctive ordering with the vowel assimilation rule R 14 (5.1.5 (g)), then the variant form *weesDa* 'pray!' (plural) can also be accounted for. /we-is-åD-a/→ /weesaDa/ → *wêesDa*. Again there is phonological motivation from the 2 C constraint.

Morphophonemic processes are limited to the general cases (1) where a vowel-final extension prefixes a vowel-initial root and (2) where a consonant final extension prefixes a consonant-initial root.

From such examples as (51) it is clear that assimilation of vowels does not occur for some prefix extensions. This could be marked in the lexicon.

(51)   'I came down'   *a-só-eeg-e*   (Focus-Ext-Root-Aspect)
       'I came off'   *ka-só-eeg-e*   (Ext.-Ext.-Root-Aspect)
       'we went together'   *is-le-irånn-e*   (Ext.-Ext.-Stem-Aspect)

There are other morphemes, as in (52), where vowel-assimilation does take place.

(52)   'I came from'   /ka-imi/   →   *kími*   (NB Class 1 verb)
       'you came from'   /ka-t-imi/   →   *katími*
       'I scratched with'   /ka-ooxe/   →   *kóoxe*
       'I went from'   /ka-irDe/   →   *kíirDe*

Here a simple assimilation rule is required.

The only consonant-final extension known is the simple reflexive *is-*. When *is-* is followed by the prefix extension *le-*, there is a fusion in normal speech:

R 20. s + l → $ł$

Some data is given below:

(53)   'we became friends (together)'   *ál-is-lê-n-itaH*   (NB Class 1) (*ál* = 'friend')
       'they went together'   *is-lê-írten*

5.5. The Reduplicative (Heine's Frequentative).

The root-initial syllable reduplicates forming an intensive which semantically is indicative of repeated, prolonged, or intensive action.

(54)   **Reduplicative**
       'I shivered'[59]   *a-Harme*   *a-HaHårme*
       'I hit'   *a-gudde*   *a-gugûdde*
       'I escaped'   *a-firDe*   *a-fifírDe*

This is accounted for by a rule roughly formulated as R 21:

R 21. **Reduplication** ϕ → $C_i V_j$ $\Big/ \left[\dfrac{\overline{\qquad}}{<\text{RED}>} \right] C_i V_j$

---

[59] In these examples *a-* is a focus marker, marking [+ pred. focus] see Oomen (1977).

In vowel-initial roots a glottal closure separates the reduplicated vowel from the root vowel.

			Reduplicative
(55)	'I saw'	*árge*	*aʾárge*
	'you saw'	*ágarte*	*aʾágarte*

The focus marker *a-* assimilates to the root-initial vowel, with loss of length.

The reduplicative forms are subject to a contraction process in the case of consonant-initial roots.

(56)		**Reduplicative forms**		
	'I shivered and shivered'	*a-HaHárme*	~	*a-HHárme*
	'I hit and hit'	*a-gugúdde*	~	*a-ggúdde*
	'I escaped and ran off'	*a-fifírDe*	~	*a-ffírDe*

As illustrated in (56), this leads to a surface form with a geminated root-initial consonant. This is a surface regularity which is not permitted in underlying lexical forms in Rendille, where clustering is only permitted medially between vowels. This is not unexpected, if the sequence "consonant plus boundary" is taken as significant for the 2 C constraint. In addition, the contraction can only occur when the form surfaces with a vowel-final morpheme prefixed to the stem. Thus, the forms in (56) above are prefixed by a focus marker. V-deletion readily accounts for these contracted forms, and it is rather the conspiratorial nature of the solution that is of interest.

The V-deletion rule can only accept as input those forms which are themselves the result of the reduplication process and indeed only the subset of those which are prefixed by a vowel-final morpheme. (Thus for instance, the focus marker must be attached to the verb of the clause before this deletion can take place.)

When the root vowel which is to be reduplicated is long, the vowel in the reduplicative is nevertheless short.

(57)				
	'he ate and ate'	*a-ñañâame*	~	*a-ññâame*
	'he spoke and spoke'	*a-yeyêeDe*	~	*a-yyêeDe*
	'he pulled and pulled'	*a-jijîite*	~	*a-jjîite*

6. IMPERATIVE AFFIRMATIVE FORMS

For simple stem verbs, the root itself is the imperative singular, and a suffixed vowel *a* is the plural marker.

(58)		**Sg.**	**Pl.**
	'give birth!'	*Del*	*Dêla*
	'burn it!'	*gub*	*gûba*
	'choose!'	*saH*	*sáHa*
	'send!'	*êreg*	*êrga*
	'mix!'	*wǒras*	*wǒrsa*

Reflexive-middle stems take *o* suffixed to the root in singular and *âD* suffixed to the root in plural with the plural marker *a* following.

(59)   **Sg.**   **Pl.**
    'catch!'   *xåbo*   *xåbDa*
    'smile!'   *mûso*   *mûsDa*
    'sing!'   *gînnaano*   *ginnåanDa*
    'stand!'   *tôlosso*   *tolossåDa*   (cp. simple stem forms
                                                tolol, tolola)
    'warm yourself!'   *DaHamóo*   *DaHamóoDa*

The varying forms of the reflexive-middle *åD* in the plural are governed by the same morphophonemic processes discussed in 5.1.5 above. Sasse (1976) has a brief reference to the similarity of imperative singular forms of the reflexive-middle in Somali, Rendille and Daasenech. He (correctly, in my opinion) treats the reflexive-middle as having zero realization in the singular, with *o* as the singular marker vowel. This is supported by comparison with Konso:

(60)   **Sg.**   **Pl.**
    'go!' (for own benefit)   *aanaDo*   *aanaDa*

Causative stems take *i* suffixed to the root in singular, and *îc* suffixed to the root in plural with the plural marker *a* following.

(61)   **Sg.**   **Pl.**
    'dry it!'   *ångagi*   *angagîce*
    'swallow!'   *xôrxei*   *xorxeyca ~ xorxiica*
    'fry it!'   *Daî*   *Daîca*
    'feed!'   *golli ~ góloli*   *gollíca ~ gololíca*
    'cook!'   *kåri*   *kårca*

Again the surface forms in the plural are governed by the restrictions dealt with in 5.3. Here as with the reflexive-middle, the causative has zero realization in singular forms, which take the singular marker vowel *i*.

The table in (62) summarizes the forms of the imperative.

(62)   **sing.**   **plur.**
    simple stems   ϕ   *-a*
    reflexive-mid.   *-o*   *-åD-a*
    causative   *-i*   *-îc-a*

7. NEGATIVE FORMS OF THE VERB

In general, negative forms require both a prefix and a suffix. It is convenient to consider the prefix first.

7.1. The Negative Prefix.

This has various forms, depending on mood or aspect, as shown in (63). Relevant data will be found in section 7.2.

(63)		
	negative perfect	*ma-*
	negative imperfect	*ma-*
	negative imperative	*a-*
	negative subjunctive	*i-*

When the following root is vowel-initial, then these prefix vowels assimilate completely to the root vowel. Their mora value is retained, the assimilation resulting in a long vowel. In cases where the root-initial vowel is itself long, the assimilated sequence is adjusted to produce a surface vowel of two morae in length.

(64)	'...didn't go in'	*masógilin*	←	/ma-só-gil-n/
	'...didn't cry'	*móoyin*	←	/ma-óoy-n/

A V-assimilation rule of the general form of R 14 is required. If a surface constraint is assumed, prohibiting vowel sequences of three morae in length, as in (65), then a rule R 22 is required to remove violations of this constraint, such as that arising from /ma-ooy-n/ noted in (64) above.

(65)   *VVV

R 22. $V_i V_i V_i$ → $V_i V_i$,   governed by (65)

7.2. The Negative Suffix.

7.2.1. Imperative Mood.

It is simpler to consider this mood first, as exemplified below:

(66)		**sing.**	**plur.**	
	'don't push it!'	*atáxin*	*ataxína*	(simple stem)
	'don't catch it!'	*axabán*	*axabánna*	(refl-mid)
	'don't cook it!'	*akarín*	*akarínna*	(causative)

As will appear, it is better to consider that the simple stem negative imperative is composed of the negative suffix -*n*, followed in plural forms by the marker vowel -*a*. The vowel *i* associated with the negative suffix in simple stems is considered to be epenthetic, resulting from the non-occurrence of word-final consonant clusters in surface forms.

The movement of the high tone from root to the following stem vowel in the plural forms of simple stems would require a rule of the general form

R 23. $(_{RÓOT})$ $(\quad)$ $\rightarrow$ $(_{ROOT})$ $(\;'\;)$

The general features of this analysis allow the surface features of derived stem forms to be readily accounted for. The derivation of a reflexive-middle and a causative stem are shown below in (67) and (68) respectively.

		Sg.	Pl.
(67)	'don't catch it!'	/a-xáb-áD-n/	/a-xáb-áD-n-a/
	R 23: tone deletion	/a-xab-áD-n/	/a-xab-áD-n-a/
	R 7: *n*-assimilation	/a-xab-án-n/	/a-xab-án-n-a/
	surface form	*axabán*	*axabánna*

Since the final *n* in the singular forms is not long phonetically, a degemination rule is required.[60] Thus:

R 24. $\begin{bmatrix} C \\ +\,gem \end{bmatrix}$ $\rightarrow$ $[\,\text{-gem}\,]$ $/$ ____   #

This rule is phonotactically motivated by the 2 C constraint[61] and is ordered to follow the various assimilation rules.

		Sg.	Pl.
(68)	'don't cook it!'	/a-kár-íc-n/	/a-kár-íc-n-a/
	R 23: tone deletion	/a-kar-íc-n/	/a-kar-íc-n-a/
	R 17: *n*-assimilation	/a-kar-ín-n/	/a-kar-ín-n-a/
	surface forms	*akarín*	*akarínna*

Once more the degemination rule is operative.

A comparison of the following is instructive:

(69)		Sg.	Pl.
	'don't be happy!' (simple stem)	*aHamáaDin*	*aHamaaDína*
	'don't amuse him!' (causative)	*aHamaaDín*	*aHamaaDínna*

There is a close interaction among tone, gemination, and assimilation and a strong dependence on the 2 C constraint.

---

[60] Present data has no forms where a negative imperative singular is suffixed by a vowel. If that should be possible, then this analysis predicts that the gemination is realized in surface forms. If it is assumed instead that the reflexive-middle is a zero form here, as is the case in the corresponding affirmative forms, then it is difficult to account for the *a* vowel following the root.

[61] There is motivation here for treating C-clusters and C-geminates differently. According to the general position adopted here, final C-clusters are subject to vowel epenthesis, whereas final C-geminates are subject to degemination.

7.2.2. Perfect Aspect.

This is a non-inflecting form.

(70) '...didn't push'   *matåxin*   (simple stems)
      '...didn't pull'   *majíitin*
      '...didn't scratch'   *móoxin*   ←   /ma-óox-n/
      '...didn't turn'   *mùurgiin*   ←   /ma-úrgii-n/

      '...didn't catch'   *maxåban*   (reflexive-middles)
      '...didn't marry'   *maDísan*

      '...didn't cook'   *makårin*   (causatives)
      '...didn't trip up'   *makùfin*

A suffix of form *-n* is suggested here also, and derivations are similar to those proposed for the negative imperatives immediately above.

Here the high tone remains on the root. With vowel-initial roots a tone rule of the general form of R 25 is required.

R 25.   VV́   →   V́V

7.2.3. Imperfect Aspect.

Here the negative forms include the block element and so result in a full paradigm.

(71) | | simple stem | reflexive-middle | causative |
      | | *tåx-* 'push' | *xåb-* 'catch' | *jíb-* 'break' |
      | 1st | *matåxo* | *maxåbDi* | *majíbco* |
      | 2nd | *matåxto* | *maxåbatti* | *majíbisso* |
      | 3rd m. | *matåxo* | *maxåbti* | *majíbco* |
      | f. | *matåxto* | *maxåbatti* | *majíbisso* |
      | 1st pl. | *matåxno* | *maxåbanni* | *majíbinno* |
      | 2nd | *matåxtan* | *maxåbattan* | *majíbissan* |
      | 3rd | *matåxan* | *maxåbtan* | *majíbcan* |

Assimilations are as already covered for affirmative forms of the verb. The most obvious surface feature is the occurrence of the marker vowel *o* with simple stems and causatives, with reflexive-middle stems taking the marker vowel *i*. Attention has been drawn in 5.1.5 (c) to the fact that this same alternation is found for reflexive-middle stems in the subjunctive aspect.

7.2.4. Subjunctive Aspect.

The subjunctive negative, occurring in subordinate verbs, relative clauses, and jussives—in this last case apparently without the negative prefix—is a non-inflecting form.

(72)	'live'	*ijîrin*			(simple stems)
	'push'	*itâxin*			
	'go'	*îran*	←	/i-ír-áD-n/	(reflexive-mid)
	'cook'	*ikårin*	←	/i-kár-íc-n/	(causative)

The derivations and rules already employed cover these data also.

A focus marker suffixed to these forms reveals gemination of the final *n* predicted by this analysis for reflexive-middle and causative stems. Thus:

(73)	'Because I didn't go...'	*id an îranne*	/i-ír-áD-n-e/ (-*e* is focus marker)
	'Because I didn't cook food...'	*id an gólol ikårinne*	/i-kár-íc-n-e/
	'Because I didn't push...'	*id an itâxine*	/i-táx-n-e/

8. VERBAL NOUNS[62]

In constructions such as those in (74) there are three possible forms of verbal noun, not all of which necessarily occur for any particular root.

(74)   'I want to go'
           'I came to see you'
           'Stealing (= to steal) is bad'
           'My fear of lions is great (= my fearing of lions is great)'
           'My going is tomorrow (= I am going tomorrow)'

The various forms, which are non-varying, are illustrated in (75). No discernible difference in meaning between the forms has been noted.

(75)   i.   *nasm-e* ⎫
              nasîn-e ⎬ *doona*   'I want to rest' (-*e* is focus marker)
              nasnân-e ⎭

        ii. *ati argín-e* ⎫
              ati arginân ⎬ *kiimi*   'I came to see you'[63]
              argim-e ⎭

        iii. *hatnân* ⎫
              hatm-e ⎬ *a suuc*   'stealing is bad' (*a* is copula)
              hatin ⎭

---

[62] The form with suffix -*nân* is Heine's infinitive. Since there are three different forms which function similarly, a less specific label has been chosen here. Oomen (1977) also notes three forms: (1) -*nân* forms, (2) forms similar to negative imperative singular or negative past, (3) forms similar to negative present. Her (2) and (3) she suggests are subjunctive forms, present and past. Her subjunctive past is my subjunctive; her subjunctive present is my non-inflecting verbal noun form ending in -*in*.

[63] Roots which undergo contraction and/or metathesis, sporadically show two forms with -*nân*, e.g. *árginân* ~ *ágarnân* 'seeing', *gudubnân* ~ *guddinân* 'hitting', *fîrDinân* ~ *fîrinnân* 'escaping'. Roots *dâlam-* 'be ignorant', *gîsam-* 'share', *bólox-* 'feel pain', show the respective forms *dâlminân*, *gîsnân*, *bólxinân* only.

The idiosyncrasy of occurrence is plain. The relationship of these forms to each other and to noun and verb is elusive. Both of these factors speak against viewing the forms as primarily verbal in nature. On the other hand, they are not simple nouns either! For this reason I suggest the term "verbal noun" to cover all forms together. This is schematized in (76):

(76)	**Noun**	**Verbal Noun**	**Verb**
	'fear'	'fearing'	'I feared'
	korór	*kororín*	*koróre*
		korornân/kororrân	

Rendille exhibits a "possessed verbal noun" ('my coming, my going...') as is typical of Afroasiatic languages, e.g. Konso, Amharic.

(77)   'my going is tomorrow'   *irântey*   *a*   *saHata*
                                        /ir-áD-n-t-ey/[64]

In structure this is Verbal Noun + Gender Marker + Possessive Suffix. Either the feminine marker *t* or the masculine *k* can be used with suitable roots. Full paradigms are given in (78).

(78)		'my going', etc.	cf. Class 1 verb: 'my coming', etc.
	1st	*irantey*	*imaatnankey*
	2nd	*irantaH*	*imaatnankaH*
	3rd m.	*irantis*	*imaatnankis*
	3rd f.	*irantice*	*imaatnankice*
	1st in.	*iranten*	*imaatnanken*
	1st ex.	*iranteño*	*imaatnankeño*
	2nd pl.	*irantin*	*imaatnankin*
	3rd pl.	*irantico*	*imaatnankico*

As can be seen below, at least two verbal noun forms can be possessed in this way, and also take the relative marker:

(79)   'my fearing of lions is great'   *korornanteyti* ⎫
                                                kororinteyti   ⎬   *baHasi a miig*

The structure of the underlying form /koror-nân-t-ey-ti/ is "root + V/noun marker + gender + possessive + relative marker".

---

[64] Apparently the only verbal noun form for this root is *iran*, which is presumably derived from underlying /ir-aD-n/.

Possessed verbal nouns can appear in either nominative or accusative case. The deleted agent form, or passive, *ala* is used for the latter.[65]

(80)   'he knows my going'   *irantey agarta*
             'my going was known'   *irantey ala agarta*

In general there is no assimilation across the boundary between root and verbal noun suffix, but where the root ends in *r, m,* or *D,* there is assimilation. (See *n*-assimilations, 4.2.3.2 above.)

(81)   'resting'   *nasnân*
             'giving birth'   *Delnân*
             'escaping'   *firDinân/firinnân*
             'grinding'   *tunnân*   from /tum-/
             'fearing'   *korornân/kororrân*

The 2 C constraint is the most generally operative rule in the derivation of *-nân* forms, three consonant clusters being avoided by i-epenthesis at the morpheme boundary:

(82)   'seeing'   *arginân/agarnân*
             'breathing'   *nebsinân*
             'sending'   *erginân*

Causative and reflexive-middle morphemes are generally dropped in the formation of verbal nouns, but *kâr-* 'cook' is an exception.

(83)   'cooking'   *karisnân*
                                     karis
                                     karisime

---

[65] Heine (1976) describes constructions with *ala* as intransitives realizing an underlying agent. Prof. R. Hetzron, on comparison with Somali, suggests the gloss 'one knows my going' as preferable to 'my going was known', in which case unmarked SOV becomes the marked order OSV, without a change of case taking place.

BIBLIOGRAPHY

ANDRZEJEWSKI, B.W.
    1969.   "Some observations on hybrid verbs in Somali." *African Language Studies* 10:47-89.

BLIESE, L.
    1973.   "Notes on the reconstruction of the glottal stop in the Aussa dialect of ʿAfar." *Anthropological Linguistics* 15:373-82.

HAYWARD, R.J.
    1975.   "Middle voice verb forms in Eastern Cushitic." *Transactions of the Philological Society*, pp. 203-24.

HEINE, B.
    1976.   "Notes on the Rendille language (Kenya)." *Afrika und Übersee* 59:186-223.

HETZRON, R.
    1975.   "Where the grammar fails." *Language* 51:859-72.

HILL, J. H.
    1970.   "A peeking rule in Cupeño." *Linguistic Inquiry* 1:534-9.

OOMEN, A.J.G.
    1977.   "Aspects of Rendille grammar with special reference to focus structure." MA Thesis, Nairobi, mimeo.
    1978.   "Focus in the Rendille clause." *Studies in African Linguistics* 9:35-65.

SASSE, H-J.
    1976.   "Dasenech." In M.L. BENDER (ed.), *The Non-Semitic Languages of Ethiopia*, pp. 196-221. Michigan State University: African Studies Center.

SIM, R.J.
    1977a.   "The phonology and morphology of the word in Konso." MA Thesis, Nairobi, mimeo.
    1977b.   "A list of Rendille verbs." Nairobi, mimeo.

TUCKER, A.N.
    1967.   "Fringe Cushitic: An experiment in typological classification." *BSOAS* 30:655-80.

Monographic Journals of the Near East   *Afroasiatic Linguistics* 8/1 (May 1981)

GENDER AND PLURALITY IN RENDILLE*

Antoinette Oomen

Rijksuniversiteit te Leiden

This study contains a synchronic description of Rendille nouns and, in addition, a certain amount of internal reconstruction, supported by comparative evidence. Gender, with its associated accentual patterns, forms an important part of the paper. An analysis of the feminine form leads to the reconstruction of a feminine proto-suffix, now practically lost. The curious interplay of gender and number is discussed. Two apparently unrelated plural suffixes are shown to go back to the same proto-suffix. Patterns of agreement are presented in detail. The paper is supplemented by a list of Rendille nouns.

TABLE OF CONTENTS

*This work was supported by an NSF grant BNS77-16841 (Paul Newman, Principal Investigator) awarded to the Center for Applied Linguistics. Field data on Rendille were collected in Kenya from the end of 1976 until June 1978. Bernhard Barchuma Arbele from Korr was my principal informant, without whom this paper could not have been written. I would like to thank Paul Newman for the many stimulating discussions we had on this paper and for the important suggestions and practical advice he offered.

1. INTRODUCTION

The Rendille language is spoken by approximately 15,000 nomadic people who inhabit the arid southern part of Marsabit District in Northern Kenya. Previously published material on Rendille consists of Fleming (1964), Heine (1975/76a), Oomen (1978), and Schlee (1978), which I have not yet been able to see. Rendille, which is closely related to Somali, belongs to Lowland East, a subgroup within the widely recognized Eastern branch of the Cushitic family of East Africa (Tucker and Bryan 1956:126; Fleming 1964:83; Heine 1975/76a:178).

The aim of the study is to present a more detailed description of Rendille nouns than the one presented in Heine (1975/76a) and Oomen (1978). Gender, its marking in the basic noun, and its concord will be considered, as will plurality. Accentual patterns play an important role in the analysis presented. A salient fact about Rendille nouns is the interplay of gender and number, attested elsewhere in Cushitic. A certain amount of internal reconstruction will be attempted, supported by comparative evidence. It is hoped that this study will help to unravel the complexities of the interplay of gender and number in Lowland East Cushitic and Cushitic in general.

2. PHONOLOGICAL PRELIMINARIES

2.1. Consonants.

Rendille has 20 consonants: *b, c, d, ɖ, f, g, h, ħ, j, k, l, m, n, ny, r, s, t, w, x, y.* (The symbol *ɖ* represents a post-alveolar stop *d*). The velar and pharyngeal obstruents (*g, k, x, ħ*) and the post-alveolar stop (*ɖ*) are phonetically emphatic (pharyngealized). This feature is not phonemically distinctive although phonetically it is important, both for the pronunciation of the consonants themselves and for their influence on adjacent vowels. The symbols *c* and *j* represent voiceless and voiced palatal plosives. Phonetically they are sometimes stops and sometimes affricates, depending on positional and individual variation. The phoneme *h* occurs in very few words and is in free variation with *ϕ*, depending on the speaker, e.g.

hir	=	*ir*	'tusk' (f)	
hel	=	*el*	'get!' (imperative)	
guh	=	*gu(u)*	'year' (m)	
dáhum	=	*dáum*	'play!' (imperative)	

Word final /k/ is realized as *ħ*[1]. Note the following alternations:

iláħ (f)	'tooth'	vs.	*ilkó*	'teeth'
yéyaħ (m)	'moon'	vs.	*yeyák-k-a*	'this moon'
cf. *raħ*	'frog'	vs.	*ráħ-ϕ-a*	'this frog'

---

[1] In the body of the paper, underlying final /k/ is transcribed as it is pronounced, i.e. *ħ*. In the wordlist, it is transcribed with *H* to distinguish it from the *ħ* representing underlying /ħ/.

2.2. Vowels.

Rendille has five vowels: *i, e, a, o, u.* In Oomen (1978) the question of vowel length was neglected. Further investigation has shown that vowel length is definitely phonemic and crucial to the assignment of accent. Minimal pairs distinguished by length are:

tor (m)	'plain'	vs.	*tóor* (m)	'spear'
dub (m)	'tail'	vs.	*dúub* (m)	'turban'
gos (m)	'farm'	vs.	*góos* (m)	'molar tooth'
waráb (f)	'male sheep' (pl)	vs.	*waraáb* (f)	'water carrying camels'

Long vowels can best be viewed as sequences of two identical vowels, each being able to carry its own accent. Compare:

máar	'young male cow'	*maár*	'young female cow'

One may say on the lines of e.g. McCawley (1968) that Rendille is a mora counting syllable-language.[2]

In basic nouns the phonemic contrast in length is limited to closed syllables. Open syllables in basic words have a short vowel. Open syllables may have a long vowel, however, due to affixation of grammatical morphemes (in nouns always suffixed, in verbs prefixed or suffixed).

2.3. Accentual patterns.

In Oomen (1978:37) the matter of tone and stress was only touched upon and no adequate analysis was given. The analysis adopted here differs in important respects from the earlier description.

Rendille clearly makes use of pitch as a prosodic feature. However, in analyzing Rendille, one is confronted with exactly the problem Pike (1974:169) presents: "Given a language which has syllables with high pitch and syllables with lower pitches, on what do we base the description that the high pitched syllables are part of a tone system rather than part of a stress system?" She offers a number of criteria to distinguish a multiple stress system from a tone system, the essence being that high pitch as a contrastive feature of stress affects its environment whereas high pitch as a contrastive feature of a tone system is affected by its environment. In applying these criteria to Rendille, one would interpret the high pitch as stress, not tone.

In Rendille one finds monosyllabic words, albeit few, which are only distinguished by a difference in pitch, e.g.:

ɖaħ (m)	'rope' (mid)	vs.	*ɖàħ*	'say!' (low)
máar (m)	'calf' (falling)	vs.	*maár* (f)	'female calf' (rising)
ħéer (m)	'ox' (falling)	vs.	*ħeér* (f)	'warriors' (rising)

As such Rendille has been described by previous authors as a tone language. Note that the tone of Rendille nouns is associated with gender (see section 3). Note also that when, for example, a demonstrative is used with the noun, the high pitch is on the penultimate or the ante-penultimate, depending on the syllable weight (see Newman 1972), e.g.:

---

[2] Compare with Beja (Hudson 1973), another language which is generally said to belong to Cushitic.

ínam (m)	'boy'	vs.	*inám* (f)	'girl'	
inám-k-a	'this boy'	vs.	*inám-t-a*	'this girl'	(pen. is heavy)
cf. *gátab* (m)	'waterhole'	vs.	*gátab-ɸ-a*	'this waterhole'	(pen. is light)
doxóol (m)	'cheetah'	vs.	*doxóol-ɸ-a*	'this cheetah'	(pen. is heavy)

The hypothesis put forward in this paper is that contrastive pitch in basic nouns is caused by a lost feminine suffix in feminine nouns. Looking at the question diachronically, one may say that present-day Rendille, which at first analysis appears to be a tone language, developed out of a bound stress language, i.e. word stress was bound to the penultimate or antepenultimate, depending on syllable weight.

Everything considered it may be best to say, on the lines of McCawley (1968:135), that Rendille is a pitch-accent language. Pitch in Rendille expresses merely a location, like in Japanese, and not features of individual syllables as in a real tone language such as Chinese. If, in Rendille, the high-pitched mora is located, the pitch of the other moras is predictable. Note that the mora and not the syllable is the "unit of phonological distance" (McCawley 1968:59).

In the present paper accented moras will be marked with ′, while non-accented moras will not be marked. The main phonetic manifestation of the accent is high pitch. The impression also is that accented moras are pronounced with more intensity and are longer than unaccented moras. The length of accented moras is, however, considerably less than the length of long vowels, consisting of two moras.

Although the Rendille verb and the noun phrase as a whole are not the subject of this paper and as yet have been insufficiently investigated, evidence points into the same direction, namely, divergent synchronic accentual patterns were caused by lost affixal elements. (They may also be caused by affixation of accented morphemes.) Accent analysis of the verb phrase is, moreover, complicated by its final position in the sentence, where intonation patterns interfere.

3. GENDER

Rendille nouns distinguish two genders: masculine and feminine. Only the singular exhibits gender distinction, the opposition being neutralized in the plural. Gender in nouns denoting living beings is on the whole determined by the sex of the referent, though there are some exceptions like *galtǻam* (m) 'big unmarried girl', *lîgud* (m) 'female camel which had a stillborn young'. Gender assignment in nouns denoting inanimate objects is unpredictable on semantic grounds.

Of approximately 400 basic nouns, 207 were found to be masculine and 181 feminine, while 12 were plural. Of the 400 basic nouns, only 70 were vowel-final, of which 22 were masculine and 48 feminine.

Apart from marking on the basic noun (see section 3), gender is also marked in the determiner-demonstrative system and by verbal concord (see section 5).

3.1. Gender and accent.

In present-day Rendille, basic nouns, except monosyllabics with a short vowel and nouns ending in a vowel, are overtly marked for gender by a different accentual pattern.[3]

---

[3] These gender related accentual patterns appear to be quite similar to what has been described for Somali, e.g. by Armstrong (1934:140).

3.1.1. Masculine nouns, accent and its realization.

A masculine noun has penultimate accent, realized as high-low pitch on the last two moras. Note that for the accent assignment, moras must be counted, not syllables, because syllables may contain a short or a long vowel, i.e. one or two moras. The accent assignment will accordingly be different.

Monosyllabic nouns containing a long vowel, i.e. two moras, have an accented mora, followed by a non-accented mora, realized as a falling pitch contour:

ɖíig (m)	'blood'
góos (m)	'molar tooth'
óor (m)	'bull camel'
máar (m)	'young male cow'
tóof (m)	'snake'
wéel (m)	'child'

In polysyllabic nouns the penultimate accent is realized as (mid)-high-low. If the final syllable contains a long vowel, i.e. two moras, the realization is (mid)-high-falling. Note that no nouns were found with long vowels in open final syllables.

ínam (m)	'boy'
yéyaɬ (m)	'moon'
láɬaw (m)	'stick'
ɖábal (m)	'chin'
ɬúgum (m)	'custom'
gádar (m)	'tin'
bírlab (m)	'sword'
cílim (m)	'shilling'
wéjel (m)	'rhino'
nyáxut (m)	'child(ren)'
géri (m)	'giraffe'
áɖɖi (m)	'goat(s) and sheep'
maxábal (m)	'elder'
daɬási (m)	'fly, flies'
xoxáni (m)	'food'
warába (m)	'hyena'
burgúca (m)	'married woman's necklace'
bakéla (m)	'rabbit'
ɬabáal (m)	'ostrich(es)'
omáar (m)	'forest'
maxéer (m)	'prepared camelskin'
ɬeléem (m)	'male sheep'
sigéer (m)	'disease'

Monosyllabic nouns containing a short vowel are non-accented, and have mid pitch. The pitch of these words in isolation does not differ from the pitch of feminine monosyllabics with a short vowel.

wor (m)	'news'
sam (m)	'nose'
ɗah (m)	'rope'
lum (m)	'hole'
ɗoħ (m)	'colour'
ur (m)	'belly'
il (m)	'land'
gey (m)	'tree'
af (m)	'mouth'
kul (m)	'container'

3.1.2. Feminine nouns, accent and its realization.

A feminine noun has final accent, realized as mid-high pitch on the last two moras. With monosyllabic nouns containing a long vowel, i.e. two moras, the last mora is accented, realized as a slightly rising pitch contour:

meél (f)	'place'
miín (f)	'forehead'
seéb (f)	'leaf'
iíy (f)	'sheep'
riíy (f)	'goat(s)'

In polysyllabic nouns the final accent is realized as (mid)-mid-high:

orráħ (f)	'sun'
gasár (f)	'buffalo'
kombór (f)	'stool'
ɗaħán (f)	'arm, hand'
biħin (f)	'bow'
elél (f)	'cowry, cowries'
geléb (f)	'evening'
cilím (f)	'ticks'
maxabál (f)	'married woman'
mindaxár (f)	'intestine'

Polysyllabic feminine nouns ending in a vowel exhibit a masculine pitch pattern, namely (mid)-high-low. This fact is explained in section 3.4. (Compare Somali feminine nouns ending in -*o*, which have a similar masculine pitch pattern (Armstrong 1934:142).)

úru (f)	'axe'
áda (f)	'paternal aunt'
cínni (f)	'bee(s)'
árti (f)	'spider'
káti (f)	'urine'
dundúme (f)	'anthill'
ḥelési (f)	'liver'
kursánte (f)	'knee'

In citation form, monosyllabics containing a short vowel are non-accented and have mid pitch:

wor (f)	'well'
sam (f)	'footprint'
daḥ (f)	'centre'
il (f)	'eye'
rum (f)	'truth'
bey (f)	'lake'
ul (f)	'stick'
taf (f)	'fireplace'

3.2. Masculine versus feminine pairs to mark sex.

A small number of nouns denoting living beings mark sex by changing the accentual pattern. On the surface they form minimal pairs where the pitch pattern is the only distinctive feature. All the examples found are:

máar	'young male cow'	*maár*	'young female cow'
ínam	'boy'	*inám*	'girl'
áram	'husband'	*arám*	'wife'
nyírax	'young male camel'	*nyiráx*	'young female camel'
waḥar	'male goat'	*waḥár*	'female goat'
úrbor	'young male sheep'	*urbór*	'young female sheep'
ḥeléem	'male sheep'	*ḥeleém*	'female sheep'
sibéen	'young male goat or sheep'	*sibeén*	'young female goat or sheep'
mandáan	'male twin'	*mandaán*	'female twin'
maxábal	'elder'	*maxabál*	'married woman'

One also finds suppletive forms to indicate corresponding male and female beings. Examples:

áci	'grandfather'	*inkokó*	'grandmother'[4]
abáya	'paternal uncle'	*áda*	'paternal aunt'
waráab	'male adult sheep'	*laḥ*	'female adult sheep'
kéleḥ	'male adult goat'	*riḥíy*	'female adult goat'

---

[4] The accented final vowel is probably due to a vocative suffix *-ó*, which has replaced a non-accented final vowel.

Two nouns are epicene and show sex only in gender agreement:

waláal	'brother, sister'			
walaláya	'my brother'	vs.	*walassáya*	'my sister'
soyóoḥ	'father, mother in law'			
soyokkáya	'my father in law'	vs.	*soyoḥtáya*	'my mother in law'

3.3. Masculine versus feminine to mark singular versus plural.

A limited number of masculine nouns, most of them denoting living beings use a feminine form in the plural,[5] e.g.:

kéleḥ (m)	'male goat'	*keléḥ* (f)	'male goats'
láḥaw (m)	'stick'	*laḥáw* (f)	'sticks'

The full list and discussion will be given in section 4.2.1.

3.4. The feminine form.

Feminine nouns can be distinguished according to whether they are

a)   inherently feminine such as

orráḥ (f)	'sun'
cimbír (f)	'bird'

b)   derived, with sex specification:

inám (f)	'girl'	from *ínam* (m)	'boy'
arám (f)	'wife'	from *áram* (m)	'husband'

c)   derived, with plural connotation:

aráb (f)	'elephants'	from *árab* (m)	'elephant'
laḥáw (f)	'sticks'	from *láḥaw* (m)	'stick'

All show the same accentual pattern, namely an accented last mora, which is realized as rising, mid-high, or mid-mid-high depending on the syllabic structure. As noted above (section 3.1) feminine nouns ending in a vowel and monosyllabic feminine nouns containing a short vowel differ. Both exhibit a masculine pitch pattern, namely (mid)-high-low and mid, respectively. Masculine nouns have an accented penultimate mora, which is realized as falling, high-low or mid-high-low depending on the syllabic structure. The following historical development is presented as a hypothesis to account for the distinct accentual pattern of masculine and feminine nouns.

---

[5]   Andrzejewski (1964) terms similar plurals in Somali "subplurals": e.g.: *díbi* 'ox' vs. *dibí* 'oxen'.

Originally all nouns had penultimate accent (counting in terms of moras, not syllables), except for monosyllabic, short-vowel nouns, which were unaccented. Masculine nouns were unmarked for gender. Feminine nouns however, were marked by a feminine suffix *-et / C___ ~ *-t / V___ (which in most constructions has since been lost). When the suffix *et was added to consonant-final nouns, the accent shifted to penultimate position to comply with the normal word pattern. On the other hand, when the suffix *-t was added to vowel-final nouns, the accent did not shift, because it was already on the penultimate. The hypothetical allomorph *-t of the feminine suffix thus accounts for the masculine pitch pattern of vowel-final feminine nouns in present-day Rendille. The assumed historical development of consonant-final feminine nouns, leading to contrast in stress between present day masculine and feminine nouns, is as follows:

*qórrah+et	→	*qorráh-et	>	orráh-e	→	orráh	'sun'	
*ínam+et	→	*inám-et	>	inám-e	→	inám	'girl'	cf. *ínam* 'boy'
*árab+et	→	*aráb-et	>	aráb-e	→	aráb	'elephants'	cf. *árab* 'elephant'
*méel+et	→	*meél-et	>	meél-e	→	meél	'place'	cf. *gáal* 'camel(s)'

The assumed historical development of vowel-final feminine nouns, leading to no contrast in citation form, is as follows:

*xóna+t	→	*xóna-t	>	xóna	'nut'	cf. *ába* 'father'
*oróro+t	→	*oróro-t	>	oróro	'gourd'	cf. *bakéla* (m) 'rabbit'

The assumed historical development of monosyllabic feminine nouns with a single short vowel, leading to no contrast in citation form, is as follows:

*wor+et	→	*wór-et	>	wór-e	→	wor	'well'	cf. *wor* (m) 'news'
*il+et	→	*íl-et	>	íl-e	→	il	'eye'	cf. *il* (m) 'soil'

These monosyllabic nouns presumably lost their accent when *-e* was lost in the citation form, see section 3.4.2. As only one mora was left, there could not be any contrast with another mora. Note, however, that monosyllabic masculine and monosyllabic feminine nouns take a distinct plural suffix, where with the latter the accent surfaces, e.g.:

wor (m)	'news'		pl. *worár*	(low-high)
wor (m)	'well'		pl. *woró*	(mid-high)

The accent of the feminine noun surfaces as a secondary accent to the accent of the plural suffix *-ó* (see section 4.1.), resulting in a pitch pattern mid-high as opposed to the low-high pattern of the masculine noun with the suffix *-áC*.

Internal evidence for a lost feminine suffix *-et* and an intermediate stage *-e* is presented in section 3.4.1. and 3.4.2. Comparative evidence for the lost feminine suffix in Rendille, is presented in section 3.4.4. How feminine nouns should best be entered in the lexicon in a synchronic grammar of Rendille, is considered in section 3.4.3.

3.4.1. Genitive construction.

Feminine nouns acting as the possessor in a genitive construction take a suffix -*ét* ($\sim$ -*t* / V___),
while masculine nouns do not, e.g.:

	inám (f)	'girl'
	min-kí inam-ét	'the house of the girl'
cf.	*ínam* (m)	'boy'
	min-kí ínam	'the house of the boy'
	cimbír (f)	'bird'
	barbárre-tí cimbir-ét	'the wings of the bird'
	ħeér (f)	'warriors'
	torar-ħí ħeer-ét	'the spears of the warriors'
	aráb (f)	'elephants'
	dubab-ħí arab-ét	'the tails of the elephants'
	éyma (f)	'wild sisal' (vowel-final)
	meel-tí eyma-ᵗt	'the place of the wild sisal'

Rather than assume that *-*t* is a Proto-Lowland-East genitive affix, as Black (1974:95 and 187)[6]
does, I propose that Rendille -*ét* is a reflex of the old feminine suffix.

The survival of *et, and its accent may be explained by assuming that in this specific construction,
it was originally followed by a connecting particle, most likely -*i*-, and concord with the headnoun.[7] The
suffixal elements made -*et* the penultimate and therefore accented. I assume that these suffixal elements
were lost at the time that in Rendille the word order in the noun phrase changed from predominantly
qualifier-noun to noun-qualifier. Rendille has predominantly SOV order in the sentence. According to
Greenberg (1963:79) languages with dominant SOV order generally put modifying elements before those
modified. Both orders can be observed in the Cushitic language area, while all Cushitic languages have
dominant SOV order in the sentence.

3.4.2. The surface subject marker with feminine nouns.

Oomen (1978:41) describes a nominative suffix -*e* which only occurs on the feminine noun. Its
occurrence is further restricted in that it is only suffixed to nouns ending in a consonant and if the noun
is unaccompanied by any qualifier. Neither is it suffixed to qualifiers,[8] e.g.:

Noun by itself:

inå̊m (f)	'girl'
inå̊m-e min á-ka-jír-t̯a	'the girl is in the house'

---

[6] Black (1974:95 and 187) presents a proto-Lowland-East Cushitic genitive suffix -*t*. He gives three reflexes (Somali,
Konso, Gidole), and no distributional facts.

[7] In Beja for example (Almkvist 1881) one finds a possessor-possessed construction as follows: *or-t-i-t* de 'a girl's mother,'
where the possessor precedes possessed and the possessor *or* (f) is followed by feminine marker -*t*-, genitive marker
-*i*- and feminine concord -*t* with the head noun *de* 'mother'. Also in Agaw (Hetzron 1976:19) one finds "agreeing geni-
tives".

[8] Somali -*i* (Bell 1953:38) appears to have the same distribution as Rendille -*e* and thus may be cognate.

Feminine noun, determined:

   inam-t-í der min á-ka-jír-t-a   'the tall girl is in the house'

Feminine noun, ending in a vowel:

   xóna (f)   'nut'
   xóna min á-ka-jír-t-a   'the nut is in the house'

Other examples of feminine nouns in subject position:

   sub (f)   'mud'
   súbe á-angag-t-e   'the mud has dried'
   cimbír (f)   'bird'
   cimbíre nyáxut á-golol-is-ta   'the bird is feeding its young'
   keytúr (f)   'cat'
   keytúre cimbír á-t-igis   'the cat killed the bird'

Compare with a masculine noun in subject position:

   inam (m)   'boy'
   inam min á-ka-jír-a   'the boy is in the house'

I assume that *-e* is a reflex of the feminine suffix **et* (see section 3.4.), which was at one point reinterpreted as a feminine nominative case marker and subsequently lost in the absolute form of the feminine noun. Note in this respect, that Black (1974:95, 129) presents a Proto-Lowland-East subject marking suffix **-i*; its reflexes are found on certain classes of nouns in Saho-Afar, Somali and Dasanech (note the restricted distribution).

3.4.3. Underlying feminine form in a synchronic grammar.

The proto feminine suffix **-et* has the following reflexes:

a) *-êt* in the genitive construction.

b) *-e* in the nominative.

c) *-φ* or final accent in the absolute form of the noun.

The most economical way to account for these alternations in a synchronic grammar of Rendille appears to be the following:

   Take the surface subject form with *-e* as the underlying form, and delete the final *-e*
by rule, in the absolute case, where it does not occur. Monosyllabic short-vowel feminine
nouns are thus distinguished from the masculine monosyllabic short-vowel nouns by
penultimate accent and the suffix *-e*, e.g.:

wór-e (f)		'well'	vs.	*wor* (m)	'news'

Other consonant-final feminine nouns have the normal penultimate accent, e.g.:

meél-e (f)	'place'	vs.	*gáal* (m)	'camel(s)'
inám-e (f)	'girl'	vs.	*ínam* (m)	'boy'

Polysyllabic vowel-final feminine nouns with penultimate accent are no longer abnormal, as all feminine nouns now end in a vowel and, like all nouns, regardless of gender, have penultimate accent.

Although originally a feminine marker, the ét/⁼t in the genitive construction must at some point have been reinterpreted as a genitive case marker. This assumption is strengthened by the fact that ⁼t also occurs in the genitive of plurals in *-ó*. This ⁼t, although of different origin (see section 4.1.1.2.), has also been reinterpreted as a genitive case marker. It is further assumed that the reinterpretation of *-e* as a feminine nominative case marker caused the loss of *-e* in the absolute case form. In our proposal, then, ⁼t is a genitive case marker, entered by rule, while *-e* is part of the underlying feminine form, entered in the lexicon.

On the basis of the foregoing, all feminine consonant-final nouns are entered with *-e* in the appendixed wordlist, while the citation forms are continued to be used in the body of the paper.

3.4.4. Comparative evidence.

For Rendille a feminine marker **-et* has been reconstructed. The reconstruction was based on internal evidence; there is also abundant comparative evidence.

Reflexes of a Proto-Cushitic feminine formative **-Vt*, presumably ultimately derived from Proto-Afroasiatic, are found throughout the Cushitic family (see a.o. Castellino 1975). Examples are:

a) Inside Lowland-East Cushitic:

Gidole (Black 1974:297)

luk-ket (f)	'leg, foot'	cf. Rendille: *luḳ* (f)	'leg, foot'

Galab (Sasse 1974:413)

làf-ìtì (f)	'bone'	cv. Rendille: *laf* (f)	'bone'

Bayso (Hayward 1979:106)

ariiti (f)	'sun'	cf. Rendille: *orráḳ*	'sun'

Somali (Bell 1953:71)

shimbir (f)	'bird'	and *dal shimbireed*	'a fledgeling'

Note that in Somali (Abraham 1964:262) feminine nouns have an accentual pattern similar to what we have observed in Rendille, e.g.:

ínan	'son'	vs. *inán*	'daughter'

In Afar (Colizza 1887:66) one finds:

> *bála*   'boy'   vs. *balá*   'girl'   (note stress opposition)

In Konso (Black 1974:126) one also finds feminine nouns which are accented on the final root vowel, e.g.:

> *hilt-eéta*   'fig tree'   (plus additional feminine suffix)

b) Outside Lowland-East:

Beja (Almkvist 1881:59)

> *tak*   'man'   vs. *takat*   'woman'

In Bilin (Hetzron 1976:15) *t* appears only after feminine nouns preceding an ablative or directive (but *not* with genitive as in Rendille and Somali; this is additional evidence that *-et* originally was not a genitive marker!):

> *dexna-led*   'from an old man' vs. *dexna-te-led*   'from an old woman'

In Awngi (Hetzron 1976:15) the feminine singular is consistently marked *-a.*

Kambata (Grover Hudson 1976:251) ordinarily employs a feminine suffix *-ta* with the absolute form, e.g. *adancuta* (f) 'cat'.

Note that one archaic Rendille construction was found, used in prayers where *-ât* (not *-êt*) was found suffixed to 2 feminine consonant-final nouns in the genitive case:

> *wax-í serey-át icow il-át*   'the God of the sky and the earth'

It is probably safe to posit a Proto-Cushitic feminine formative **-at.*

4. NUMBER

Most Rendille nouns have a distinct plural form, although there are many nouns which have one form only. The latter will be discussed in section 4.2.2. and 4.3.1. Heine (1975/76a:194) and Oomen (1978:42) have described approximately the same plural suffixes, although their descriptions of a number of individual nouns and their respective plural suffixes differ. Further analysis of Rendille nouns and comparative evidence suggest a more accurate analysis. Plural suffixes which on first view seem unrelated will be shown to go back to the same proto-plural suffix, while another plural suffix will be shown to be a variant of the feminine suffix *-et.*

4.1. The plural suffixes -áC and -ó.

4.1.1. The plural suffix -áC.

The plural suffix -áC occurs on monosyllabic masculine nouns with long or short vowel, i.e. -á is suffixed and the final consonant is reduplicated. The phonetic realization of the accent is low/falling-high, e.g.

tor	'plain'	pl:	*torár*
jit	'road'	pl:	*jitát*
sam	'nose'	pl:	*samám*
óor	'bull camel'	pl:	*óorár*
tóor	'spear'	pl:	*tóorár*

Two monosyllabic feminine nouns have been recorded, which take -áC. These are

meél	'place'	pl:	*méelál*
ḥaán	'water container'	pl:	*ḥaanán*

Note that polysyllabic masculine nouns do not take the -áC plural suffix. Rather they take a plural suffix -Ce (see section 4.2.), or, by exception, -ó (see section 4.1.2.).

4.1.2. The plural suffix -ó.

The plural suffix -ó occurs on monosyllabic and polysyllabic feminine nouns. After a final vowel the suffix is -yó. The phonetic realization of the accent is (mid)-mid-high, e.g.

kob	'shoe'	pl:	*kobó*
kur	'hill'	pl:	*kuró*
sirír	'bed'	pl:	*siriró*
kombór	'stool'	pl:	*komboró*
aḍáḥ	'back'	pl:	*aḍaḥó*
írti	'bead'	pl:	*irtiyó*
ḍowóḥo	'jackal'	pl:	*ḍowoḥoyó*

-ó was also found with the following masculine nouns (complete list), in one case in free variation with -áC:

gey	'tree'	pl:	*geyó* or *geyáy*
raḥ	'frog'	pl:	*raḥó*
far	'finger'	pl:	*faró*
díri	'pot'	pl:	*diriyó*
náḥas	'breast'	pl:	*naḥasó*
fólas	'male camel'	pl:	*folasó*
jílib	'knee'	pl:	*jilibó*

útaħ	'goatskin'	pl:	uktó
máar	'male calf'	pl:	maaró 'calves' (either sex)
nyírax	'young male camel'	pl:	nyirxó
wáħar	'male goat'	pl:	waħaró
úrbor	'young male sheep'	pl:	urboró
mandáan	'male twin'	pl:	mandaanó

Note that the last five of these masculine nouns have feminine counterparts, e.g.

| máar | vs. | maár | 'male calf' | vs. | 'female calf' |

In these cases the form of the plural is best explained by assuming that the plural is based upon the feminine singular form.

In a number of the nouns which take -ó, the vowel of the final syllable is elided. All the examples found are as follows:

karám	'small calabash'	pl:	karmó
arít	'gate'	pl:	artó
nyírax	'young male camel'	pl:	nyirxó
nyiráx	'young female camel'	pl:	nyirxó
geléb	'evening'	pl:	gelbó
jílib	'knee'	pl:	jilbó
iláħ	'tooth'	pl:	ilkó
ħeléem	'male sheep'	pl:	ħelmó
ħeleém	'female sheep'	pl:	ħelmó
ilím	'tear'	pl:	ilmó
nabáħ	'ear'	pl:	nabħó

In all cases, except the last, the liquid in penultimate consonant-position seems to be the conditioning factor. This statement is also borne out by analysis of verb forms.

In five nouns, the vowel dropping was accompanied by metathesis of the last two consonants:

baħáb	'armpit'	pl:	babħó
útaħ	'goatskin'	pl:	uktó
ugár	'skinbag'	pl:	urgó
đafár	'cloth'	pl:	đarfó
abár	'mother'	pl:	arbó

The metathesis is triggered off by a liquid in final position. The examples with final ħ (/k/) and b are unusual, although another example of metathesis involving a pharyngeal fricative and a bilabial has been found:

| aħam | 'eat!' (singular) | vs. | amħa | 'eat!' (plural) |

The plurals in *-åC* and *-ó* take plural agreement. For example, they use the plural marker *k* and they require plural verbal concord (see section 5).[9] These forms thus differ from other "plurals" (see section 4.3.) which take feminine concord.

4.1.3. Plural nouns, not ending in *-åC* or *-ó*.

A few nouns were found which take plural agreement but do not end in *-åC* or *-ó*. In all cases the accent falls on the last syllable. They do not have a singular counterpart.

They are the following:

biná	'wild animals'	(note *-á*)
kolá	'domesticated animals'	(note *-á*)
bicé	'water'	cf. Somali: *bíyyó* (pl)
kaanú	'milk'	cf. Somali: *ćáanó* (pl)
incabá	'maize'	(probably loan)
sonxór	'sugar'	(loan)
marát	'brains'	(note *-át*)
dúubát	'fog'	(note *-át*)
banáy	'light'	(see section 4.2.1.)
anxád	'lightning'	(deverbative)
sombób	'lungs'	cf. Somali: *sámbáb* 'lung'
basbás	'different kinds of milk mixed'	(note complete reduplication)

4.2. Hypothetical proto plural suffix *-åt*.

There is evidence to suggest that both plural suffixes *-åC* and *-ó* go back to the same proto plural suffix *-åt*.

4.2.1. *åC* < *-åt*.

a) When a plural noun ending in *-åC* is determined, that is when the plural marker *-k-* (see section 5.1.) is suffixed, the realization of final *-C* + *-k* is always *-ss-*, independent of the form of the *-C*, e.g.

jitát	'roads'	*jitássa*	'these roads'
óorár	'male camel'	*óorássa*	'these male camels'
samám	'noses'	*samássa*	'these noses'
lafáf	'bones'	*lafássa*	'these bones'
dakák	'ropes'	*dakássa*	'these ropes'
minán	'houses'	*minássa*	'these houses'

A rule *t* + *k* → *ss* is natural, *t* assimilating to *k* in fricativeness and *k* assimilating to *t* in place of articulation. A rule such as *m* + *k* → *ss* (as in *samamka* → *samassa*) however, is very unnatural. This fact is a good argument for assuming that C < *t*.

---

[9] Heine (1975/76a:194) says that some of the plurals in *åC* are feminine, but I have not found any.

b) One plural noun was found not ending in a reduplicated consonant, which also showed -ss-, when determined:

    banáy   'light'   *banássa*   'this light'

It is assumed that *banáy* < *banât*. Compare a similar process of **t/*d* > *y* in Somali—Rendille correspondences: *bad* (*d* voiceless in word final position) vs. *bey* 'sea — lake' (f); *geed* vs. *gey* 'tree' (m).

c) Plurals in -*âC* do not take -*t* in the genitive construction as do plurals in -*ó* (see section 4.1.1.2.) presumably because the -*t* is already there, although disguised as -C, e.g. *dubas-sî oorâr* 'the tails of the male camels'.

4.2.2. -*ó* < **-â* < **-ât*.

The main evidence for -*ó* going back to a form ending in -*t* is the following: plural nouns ending in -*ó* add -*t* when acting as possessor in a genitive construction, e.g.

    cimbír   'bird'   pl: *cimbiró*
    barbárre-tí cimbirót   'the wings of the birds'
    gey   'tree'   pl: *geyó*
    liximó-hí geyót   'the branches of the trees'

Since originally Rendille did not have a -*t* genitive marker (see section 3.4.1.), the final -*t* that is added, must originally have been part of the plural noun stem.

The survival of -*t* in the plural possessor nouns can be explained in the same way as the -*t* surviving in the feminine possessor nouns, namely by assuming that it originally was followed by a genitive suffix **-i* plus concord. The -*t* suffixed in plural possessor nouns is, however, not the same -*t* as that suffixed to feminine possessor nouns. The former goes back to an accented plural suffix **-ât*, the latter to a non-accented feminine suffix **-et*.

It is assumed that at a very early period the -*t* was lost in the citation form and the vowel changed from **-â* to -*ó*.[10] The question is how to account for the distribution of the present-day plural forms -*ó* (< **-â*) and -*âC*, both presumably going back to **-ât*.

In a synchronic analysis the choice between the two forms seems to be determined to a great extent by gender (see section 4.1.). I would suggest that the historical explanation for the distribution of the plural suffixes is phonological. -*âC* was originally limited to monosyllabic nouns, while the non reduplicated form was used with polysyllabic nouns. This would account for the fact that -*âC* is only used with monosyllabic masculine nouns, while polysyllabic masculine nouns use another suffix -*Ce* (see section 4.3.). For feminine nouns, some of which now are monosyllabic in citation form, we assume that the plural suffix was preceded by the feminine suffix and that feminine "monosyllabic" nouns were in fact polysyllabic and thus required -*ó* and not -*âC*, e.g. **wôr-et-ó* (now *woró*) 'wells', cf. **wor-âC* (now *worâr*) 'news'. We assume then that in the hypothetical form **wôr-et-ó*, *e* was dropped and *t* weakened to *y*, which itself was later lost with nouns ending in a consonant. Evidence for this weakening of *t*, is found in one plural noun in Rendille:

    ir (f)   'tusk'   pl: *iryó*

---

[10]Plurals in -*a* are found all over Cushitic, e.g. Beja, Sidamo, Afar-Saho. The change from **-â* to -*ó* is also found in Somali. The exact condition for this change is unclear, e.g. Somali *kab* (f) 'shoe' pl: *kabó*, cf. Rendille *kob* (f) 'shoe' pl: *kobó*.

and in Jabarti (Von Tiling 1921/22:105):

far (f)	'finger'	pl:	*fár-nya* (with epenthetic nasal)

Further evidence for the positing of feminine *-et-* preceding plural suffix in feminine nouns is as follows:

a) In feminine vowel-final nouns the plural suffix is *-eyð*, where *-e-* replaces the final vowel, assimilating to the *y*, e.g.

áda	'paternal aunt'	pl:	*adeyó*
úru	'axe'	pl:	*ureyó*
kórro	'camel bell'	pl:	*korreyó*

I assume that *-y-* here, is not epenthetic, but is a reflex of feminine *-t-*. If it were epenthetic, one would have expected *-w-* between rounded vowels, and not *-y-*.

b) The different accentual pattern of plurals in *-åC* and *-ó*, e.g. *wor-år* (low-high) 'news' vs. *worð* (mid-high) 'wells'. It is thought that in the first example the low-high pitch is the realization of the unaccented masculine noun plus accented plural suffix, and the mid-high pitch in the second example the realization of the accented feminine noun (accent caused by the feminine suffix) plus the accented plural suffix.

To account for the plural possessor noun in *-ót* and not expected *-át*, it is proposed that at one point the *-t* by itself was reinterpreted as a genitive marker (cf. section 3.4.3.). Then the vowel *-å* was reinterpreted as the plural marker and became *-ó* by analogy with plurals in *-ó*.

4.3. The plural suffix -Ce.

Polysyllabic masculine nouns generally form their plural by suffixing *-Ce*,[11] or after nouns ending in a vowel *-nye*, see exceptions in section 4.1. and see section 4.3.1. The penultimate mora becomes accented:

xóxom	'club'	pl:	*xoxómme*
dábal	'chin'	pl:	*dabálle*
míris	'cloud'	pl:	*mirísse*
urúub	'milk container'	pl:	*uruúbbe*
maxábal	'elder'	pl:	*maxabálle*
yahási	'crocodile'	pl:	*yahasínye*
dúlbe	'roofmat'	pl:	*dulbénye*

All the nouns which have this type of plural formation, are masculine. It is a productive plural formation. The plurals in *-Ce* and *-nye* all take the feminine marker *-t-* in determiner-demonstrative constructions and feminine verbal concord (see section 5.3.). Grammatically speaking, they are thus feminine singulars, not plurals. They do not add *et*, when possessor in a genitive construction:

---

[11] C is noun-final consonant reduplicated.

banay-hí bakálle	'the light of the stars'
meel-tí dulbénye	'the place of the roofmats'

4.3.1. Masculine nouns which use a pure feminine form in the plural.

A limited number of masculine nouns, most of them denoting living beings, use a pure feminine form in the plural (see section 3.3.). The full list is:

midir	'big boy'	pl:	*midír*	
galtáam	'big girl'	pl:	*galtaám*	
árab	'elephant'	pl:	*aráb*	
fárat	'horse'	pl:	*farát*	
éhel	'donkey'	pl:	*ehél*	
kéleh	'male goat'	pl:	*keléh*	
waráab	'male sheep'	pl:	*waraáb*	
óor	'male camel'	pl:	*oór*	(male, water carrying camels)
dufáan	'big male camel'	pl:	*dufaán*	
dágah	'stone'	pl:	*dagáh*	
láhaw	'stick'	pl:	*laháw*	
wéjel	'rhino'	pl:	*wejél*	
héer	'ox'	pl:	*heér*	(warriors)[12]

All of these nouns indicating plural, show *-t-* when determined and feminine verbal concord. All of the nouns show *-e*, when subject and *-et*, when possessor:

arábe wór á-ka-jír-t-a	'the elephants are at the well'
dubab-hí arabét	'the tails of the elephants' (b + h → ss)

4.3.2. Feminines with one form only.

Besides those feminines like *aráb* 'elephants' which have a masculine singular counterpart, feminines with plural connotation are found, which do not have a masculine singular counterpart, e.g.

maxál	'young sheep and goats'
cínni	'bees'
rirím	'termites'
cilím	'ticks'
márti	'strangers, visitors'
iíy	'sheep'

If one wants to specify 'one', a singulative device is used:

martí-t-o	'a stranger'	(feminine marker + indefinite pronoun)

---

[12] The word *heér* presumably originally meant 'oxen' but was extended figuratively to refer to 'warriors'. For the same semantic derivation cf: *máar* 'male calf' vs. *maár* 'female calf' vs. *máarát* 'big boy(s), but younger than the warriors; they will be the next set of warriors'.

I assume that these feminine nouns lost their masculine singular counterpart.

Of these feminine nouns with plural connotation, only *cînni* 'bees' and *mârti* 'strangers' do not take -*t* when possessor. Note the double consonant in *cînni* and the -*t* in *mârti*. These two may be grouped with the "plurals" in -*Ce*, while the others are pure feminine.

4.3.3. Hypothetical feminine suffix *-et* ~ *-te*.

If we can assume that at some point *-et* had a variant *-te*, we can analyze -*Ce* (- *nye*/V___) as going back to *-te*. In the allomorph *nye*, *y* is the reflex of *t* and *n* is an epenthetic nasal, else-where attested in synchronic analysis (see allomorphs of focus marker in Oomen (1978:51), also adjacent to *y*). Note that the accent pattern is in line with this proposal. Note that these feminine plurals in -*Ce* do not add -*t*, when possessor because the *t* is there, although disguised as C or *ny*. We see that -*te* became a productive plural suffix, but kept its feminine agreement patterns. Nouns with a pure feminine form in the plural must be considered fossilized, archaic forms, which is in line with their restricted number. Such nouns are also found in other Cushitic languages where they are also considered archaic, e.g. by Hetzron (1972:261). Examples are:

Somali (Hetzron 1972:259)	*dìbi*	'ox'	pl:	*dibí* (f)
Awngi (Hetzron 1976:15)	*birì*	'ox'	pl:	*berá* (f)
Boni (Heine 1976/77:256)	*wóol*	'rhino' pl:		*wóosh* (f)

Plural formations of other Cushitic languages are additional evidence for our proposed variant *-te*:

Sidamo (Moreno 1940:24)	*oso*	'boy' pl:	*osote*
	cf. *elo* 'lover' (m) vs. *elote* 'lover' (f)		

For Jabarti, von Tiling (1921/22:106) says that a noun may have several plural suffixes:

miŋ (m)	'house'	pl:	1	*mínne*
			2	*n.ìnnedé* (f)
ged (m)	'tree'	pl.	1	*géde*
			2	*geddedé* (f)
			3	*gédo*

The data from Jabarti suggest that originally there was a semantic difference in Cushitic between plurals adding the "plural" marker *-ât* and those adding the "feminine" marker *et/te*. This leads us to the question, why masculine singular nouns use a feminine form in the plural. In several studies on Cushitic this question is dealt with under the term "polarity".

4.4. Digression into polarity.

The concept of polarity, which was introduced in Afroasiatic studies by Meinhof (1912:18), has been discussed recently by Hetzron (1967:184).[13]   As examples Hetzron uses Somali:

---

[13] See also Hetzron (1972:259).

libàah-kii	'the lion'	pl:	*libaahyá-dii*
goól-tii	'the lioness'	pl:	*goolí-hii*

"whereby what is masculine in the singular looks feminine in the plural, and what is feminine in the singular has a masculine form in the plural." In a footnote Hetzron says that no real distinction of genders is made in the plural with regard to agreement with verbs. I would suggest that the plural *goolî-hii* is not an ordinary masculine singular form, but a distinct plural form. In Somali there are two types of plural in *-o* (Bell 1953:15, 19). One type of plural in *-o* (the corresponding singulars are masculine) takes the definitives *-ta*, etc., and the final consonants are doubled (compare Rendille "plurals" in *-Ce*). The other type (the corresponding singular is feminine) takes the definitive *-ha*, etc., and the final consonant is not doubled. Verbal concord is plural for both types. *goolî-hii* belongs to the latter type.

Therefore one cannot speak of polarity in the sense that masculine nouns become feminine in the plural and conversely feminine nouns become masculine in the plural. The first statement appears to be true but the second not. It is true that plural agreement markers show masculine characteristics, but this is a universal phenomenon, cf. section 5.1. One is then left with the fact that a number of masculine nouns take a feminine suffix to mark plurality. Note moreover that all over Cushitic the same feminine suffix is used to mark singularity. Examples are

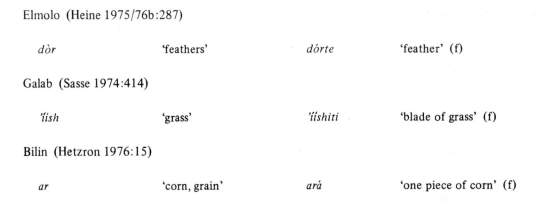

Elmolo (Heine 1975/76b:287)

    dòr   'feathers'   *dórte*   'feather' (f)

Galab (Sasse 1974:414)

    'iish   'grass'   *'iishiti*   'blade of grass' (f)

Bilin (Hetzron 1976:15)

    ar   'corn, grain'   *ará*   'one piece of corn' (f)

Perhaps one should not say that the feminine gender is used to express plurality or singularity, but to relate the two uses and say that the masculine gender, being the unmarked gender, expresses the feature [-Count], while the additional function of the feminine gender as the marked gender is to express [+Count]. [+Count] may indicate either plurality or singularity. This hypothesis is borne out by synchronic observation in 4.4.1.

4.4.1. Number-unspecified nouns in Rendille.

In addition to nouns which have a distinct plural form, there are many nouns which have one form only.[14] The feminines among those have been accounted for in section 4.3.2. The masculines can semantically be interpreted as either singular or plural, but they always show singular agreement. Examples are

---

[14] Note that, for example, in Borana (Andrzejewski 1960) the vast majority of nouns occur normally in their general form, i.e. without affixes. Plural and singulative are seldom used.

et	'man, men'
dod	'person, people'
gáal	'camel, camels'
rad	'vulture, vultures'
daḥási	'fly, flies'
gambar-tí gáal	'the hump of the camel'
cf. *gambaro-ḥí gáal*	'the humps of the camels'

These masculine nouns can be described as having the feature [-Count]. In Rendille the singulative, expressed by the feminine gender, was lost and was replaced by the following device:

rad	'vulture(s)'
rád-o	'a vulture'
rád-o kalday	'a single vulture'

while the plural, expressed by the feminine gender, became productive, i.e. it became productive for poly-syllabic masculine nouns and replaced for this group the *-ó* suffix. Those polysyllabic nouns which take the plural-suffix *-ó* (see section 4.1.) must thus be viewed as archaic or they may have changed gender. For most of these nouns, as we have seen, the plural in *-ó* is derived from their feminine counterpart, e.g.

nyírax	'young male camel'	pl:	*nyirxó*
nyiráx	'young female camel'		

It is striking in this respect that no feminine nouns were found which use the feminine form for their plural. This is so because, being feminine, they already had the feminine suffix.

5. PATTERNS OF AGREEMENT

5.1. Gender/number markers.

When a noun is modified by an adjective, a genitive, or relative clause, it is followed by a gender/ number marker plus a linking particle *-í* (in free variation with a longer form *-íye*).[15] Instead of *-í* one may have a possessive, demonstrative root, or the indefinite marker *-o*, for example,

ínam (m)	'the boy'	
ínam-k-í der	'the tall boy'	(note: *m* → *ŋ*/__velar)
ínam-k-í Korr	'the boy of Korr'	

---

[15] Numerals do not require a gender/number marker nor a linking particle. They seem moreover to control verbal agree-ment, e.g. *ínam* (m) *afar-e t-imiy* 'four boys came' (note *-e* suffixed to *afar* and feminine *t* in verb, while *ínam* is mas-culine.

ínam-k-í yimi, á der yáhe	'the boy, who came, is tall'
inám-k-aya	'my boy'
inám-k-a	'this boy'
inám-k-o	'a boy'

The gender/plural markers are as follows:

Masculine: /k/, realized as:

a) *k* after nasals and after *h* which represents underlying /k/

díim-k-a	'this tortoise'	
soyók-k-aya	'my father in law'	(*soyyóoh* 'father in law')

b) *h* after vowel:

bakéla-h-a	'this tortoise'
irbi-h-a	'this needle'

c) φ after all consonants except those mentioned under a):

dúb-a	'this tail'
díig-a	'this blood'
jít-a	'this road'
ráh-a	'this frog'

Feminine: /t/, realized as:

a) *t* after vowel and all consonants other than those mentioned under b):

xóna-t-a	'this nut'
kób-t-a	'this shoe'
bír-t-a	'this iron'
lúh-t-a	'this leg'

b) After dental and alveolar obstruents, *t* assimilates to the preceding consonant:

gaád-da	'this outfit'
oót-ta	'this fence'
hós-sa	'this grass'

If the noun ends in *l, l* combines with *t* to *ss*:

ús-sa	'this stick'	(*ul* 'stick')

Plural: /ẖ/, realized as follows:

a) *ẖ* after vowel and all consonants, except those reduplicated consonants mentioned under b):

diriyó-ẖ-a	'these pots'
biná-ẖ-a	'these wild animals'
bicé-ẖa (pl)	'this water'
bolóx-ẖ-a	'these flames'
sonxór-ẖ-a (pl)	'this sugar'

b) after plural nouns ending in *-áC* (C is noun-final consonant reduplicated), *ẖ* combines with the C to *ss*:

jitás-sa	'these roads'	(*jität*	'roads')
ɖabás-sa	'these fires'	(*ɖabáb*	'fires')
kúulás-sa	'these containers'	(*kúulál*	'containers')
minás-sa	'these houses'	(*minán*	'houses')

Historically the plural marker *ẖ* came from /k/ and the masculine/plural distinction was probably caused by a difference in following vowel. Synchronically the two consonants are clearly distinct, cf.

	jíɖ-k-a	→ *jíɖa*	'this meat' (m)
and	*anxáɖ-ẖ-a*	→ *anxáɖẖa*	'this lightning' (pl)

5.2. Demonstratives.

Demonstratives follow the noun and are preceded by one of the gender/number markers.

-a	'this, these'
-úus	'that, those'
-as	'that, those (previous reference)'

Examples:

ẖáw-t-a	'this river here'
ẖáw-t-úus	'that river over there'
ẖáw-t-as	'that river (previous reference)'

5.2.1. Independent demonstratives.

kan(a) (m)	'this one'
tan(a) (f)	'this one'
kanayó (pl)	'these ones'

kúlla (m)	'that one'
túlla (f)	'that one'
kullayó (pl)	'those ones'
kálla (m)	'that one' (pr. ref.)
tálla (f)	'that one' (pr. ref.)
kallayó (pl)	'those ones' (pr. ref.)

kan(a), etc. is used to refer to masculine nouns.
tan(a), etc. is used to refer to feminine nouns, including "plurals" with a pure feminine form and "plurals" in -C*e*/-*nye*. *kanayó*, etc. is used to refer to plural nouns ending in -*á*C and -*ó*, denoting living beings. When was referred to plurals in -*á*C and -*ó*, denoting inanimate objects, *wáh-a* 'these things', was preferred. Note that also with the independent demonstratives, we can contrast plurals in -*á*C and -*ó* with "plurals" in -C*e*/-*nye*. The latter show again feminine agreement.

5.3. Verbal concord.

There is concord in gender and number between the verb and its subject. There is no distinction of gender in the plural. In prefix-verbs (see Oomen 1978:44), masculine is marked by *y-*, feminine by *t-* and plural by *y-* ... *n*.

us á-y-imiy	'he came'
ice á-t-imiy	'she came'
íco á-y-imáten	'they came'

In suffix-verbs (Oomen 1978:45), masculine is marked by ϕ-, feminine by -*t*- and plural by ϕ ... *n*.

us á-girdám-ϕ-e	'he danced'	
íce á-girdám-t-e	'she danced'	('*m* → *n*/__*t*)
íco á-girdám-ϕ-en	'they danced'	

When a masculine noun, including those that are [-Count] , is the subject, the verb will have masculine concord:

ínam á-y-imiy	'the boy came'
gáal á-y-imiy	'the camel(s) came'

When a feminine noun, including those "plurals" with pure feminine form and those "plurals" ending in -C*e*/-*nye*, is the subject, the verb will have feminine concord:

inám-e á-t-imiy	'the girl came'
aráb-e á-t-imiy	'the elephants came'
maxabál-le á-t-imiy	'the elders came'

When a plural noun is the subject, the verb will have plural concord:

óorár á-y-imáten	'the he-camels came'
dowohoyó á-y-imáten	'the jackals came'
biná á-y-imáten	'the wild animals came'
bicé á-masáten	'the water is finished'
anxád á-masáten	'the lightning is finished'

5.4. Pronoun substitution.

Rendille pronouns of the third person are as follows:

ússu/us	'he'
íce	'she'
icó	'they' (masculine or feminine)

When a noun is the subject of the sentence, it is not followed by an agreeing pronoun as in Somali (see Hetzron 1972:259). When a pronoun refers to a previously mentioned masculine noun, it is *ússu/us*, e.g.

referring to *ínam* 'boy', *us áyimiy* 'he came'.

When a pronoun refers to a previously mentioned masculine noun,[-Count], however, there is a choice, e.g.

referring to *gáal* 'camel(s)', *us áyimiy* or *icó áyimáten*.

When a pronoun refers to a previously mentioned feminine noun, it is *íce*, e.g.

referring to *inám* 'girl', *íce átimiy*.

When a pronoun refers to a previously mentioned feminine noun, indicating plurality, there is again a choice, e.g.

referring to *aráb* elephants', *íce átimiy* or *icó áyimáten*;

referring to *maxabálle* 'elders', *íce átimiy* or *icó áyimáten*

When a pronoun refers to a previously mentioned plural noun, it is *icó*, e.g.

referring to *dowohoyó* 'jackals', *icó áyimáten*.

It appears thus that with some informants semantic plurality determines the concord in referring pronouns.

5.5. Adjectives.

Adjectives follow the noun and are preceded by a gender/plural marker + linker. They do not themselves mark gender:

ínam-k-í der	'the tall boy'	vs. *inám-t-í der*	'the tall girl'

Some adjectives show plural by complete reduplication or prefixed *a-*. They work on a simple singular/ plural system, where plural tends to be determined on semantic, not syntactic plurality:

óorassi derder/ader	'the tall bulls' (pl)
arab-tí derder/ader	'the tall elephants' (f)
maxáballe-tí derder/ader	'the tall elders' (f)

APPENDIX

INTRODUCTION

1. Transcription

1.1. Consonants and vowels.

d̠ represents the post-alveolar stop *d*. It is phonetically emphatic (pharyngealized).

c and *j* represent voiceless and voiced palatal plosives. Phonetically they are sometimes stops and sometimes affricatives, depending on positional and individual variation.

h represents the glottal fricative, is in free variation with *ϕ*, depending on the speaker.

ħ represents the pharyngeal fricative, voiceless in word-final position.

x represents the velar fricative.

Word-final /k/ is realized as *ħ*. It is transcribed with H to distinguish it from the *ħ* representing underlying /ħ/.

Length of vowels and consonants is indicated by double vowel or consonant respectively, e.g.: *aa*; *rr*.

1.2. Accent.

The accented mora is marked ´ . The accent is primarily realized by high pitch (see section 2.3.). In the case of long vowels, accent on the first vowel indicates falling pitch contour, while accent on the last vowel indicates slightly rising pitch contour. Moras following the accented mora have low pitch, moras preceding the accented mora have mid, except for plurals in -*áC*, see section 4.1. and 4.2. Therefore the moras preceding the plural suffix -*áC* will be marked ` , to distinguish them from mid-high sequences, e.g.

wòrár (p)	'news'	cf.	*woró* (p)	'wells'
sàmám (p)	'noses'	cf.	*samó* (p)	'footprints'

2. Important note

In the case of feminine nouns entered with a final -*e* (assumed underlying form, see section 3.4.3.), the final -*e* has to be deleted to arrive at the citation form. If the resultant form is monosyllabic with a short vowel, the accent also has to be effaced (see section 3.4.3.). With all the other nouns the nominative/underlying forms and the citation forms are identical.

Examples of feminine nouns entered with a final *-e* :

	inám-e	'girl'	(underlying and nominative case form)
cf.	*inám*	'girl'	(citation and accusative case form)
	wór-e	'well'	(underlying and nominative case form)
cf.	*wor*	'well'	(citation and accusative case form)

3. Abbreviations

m	masculine
f	feminine
p	plural
f (p)	feminine, i.e. showing feminine agreement, but semantically plural (see section 4.3.)

All nouns will be followed by their plural form, if they have any.

LIST OF RENDILLE BASIC NOUNS

accident	*bábul* m	*babúlle* f (p)
agegroup	*xólo* f	*xoloyó* p
animal, domesticated	*naf* m	*nàfáf* p
animals, domesticated	*ħolá* p (stock, wealth)	
——, wild	*biná* p	
ankle	*minjím-e* f	*minjimó* p
	kal m	*kàlál* p
anthill	*dundúme* f	*dundumeyó* p
antelope	*ogóor* m	*ogoórre* f (p)
arm	*daħán-e* f	*daħanó* p
armpit	*baħáb-e* f	*babħó* p
ash	*bómbey*	*bombéyye* f (p)
aunt, paternal	*áda* f	*adeyó* p
——, maternal	*íngo* f	*ingejó* p
arrow, stick	*láħaw* m	*laħáw* f (p)
arrow point	*báldo* f	*baldeyó* p
axe	*úru* f	*ureyó* p
baby, male	*ersíim* m	
——, female	*weelí beħit* m	
back	*adáħe* f	*adaħó* p
back, upper part	*kaári* f	

back, middle part	*gírgir* m	*girgírre* f (p)
back, lower part	*dub* m	*dùbáb* p
back bone	*dábar* m	*dabárre* f (p)
bag, made of skin	*ugár-e* f	*urgó* p
bag, made of skin, on the wall	*górja* f	
___ , made of cloth	*kerére* f	*kerereyó* p
bark	*nyerím-e* f	
basket	*énjel* m	*enjélle* f (p)
bead	*írti* f	*irtiyó* p
		(pl. is also: rainbow, necklace)
bed	*sirír-e* f	*siriró* p
barren female	*makán-e* f	*makanó* p
bee(s)	*cínni* f	(also: sweet)
bell, wooden camel-	*kórro* f	*korreyó* p
bird	*cimbír-e* f	*cimbiró* p
blacksmith(s)	*tumál-e* f	
blood	*đíig* m	*đíigág* p
body	*sár-e* f	*saró* p
bone	*láf-e* f	*lafó* p
book	*xadaábbe* f (p)	(is 'papers')
bottle	*iltúba* f	*iltubeyó* p
bow	*bikín-e* f	*bikinó* p
boy	*ínam* m	*yeéle* f (p)
___ , big, but not yet circumcized	*míđir* m	*miđír-e* f (p)
___ , call name	*írka*	
bracelet, metal	*kaáđ-e* f	*kaađó* p
branch	*lixím-e* f	*liximó* p
brains	*marát* p	
bread	*imkáte* f	
breast	*nákas* m	*nakasó* p
brother	*waláal* m	*walalínye* f (p)
___ , elder	*imbobó* m	*imbobínye* f (p)
		(for accented -*ó*, see footnote 4)
___ , in law	*báar* m	
buffalo	*gasár-e* f	*gasaró* p
bull	*óor* m	*óòrár* p
butter	*sikím-e* f	
calabash, spoonlike	*karám-e* f	*karmó* p
calf, male	*máar* m	*maaró* p
___ , female	*maár-e* f	*maaró* p
camel(s), general	*gáal* m	
___ , bull	*óor* m	*óòrár* p
___ , female	*áyu* f	*aló* p
___ , male castrated	*fólas* m	*folasó* p

——, big male	ɖufáan m	ɖufaán f (p)
——, pack	ħal m	oór f (p)
——, water carriers	waraáb-e f (p)	
——, young male	nyírax m	nyirxó p
——, young female	nyírax-e m	nyirxó p
——, young, but older than nyirxo	ilbór-e f (p)	
——, young, but older than ilbor-e	téru m	
——, young female, which has not yet given birth	urħál-e f	urħaló p
——, female which gave birth recently	írban m	
——, female which had a stillborn baby	lúgud m	lugúdde f (p)
——, female which is kept and milked separately	dór-e f	doró p
——, young which is being taught to carry loads	léyley m	leléyye f (p)
——, paid as dowry	cáma f	cameyó p
——, lent	máal m	
——, own property	alál-e f	alaló p
camel foot	yax m	
camel bell	kórro f	korreyó p
castrated camels or cows	sibnán-e f (p)	
cat	keytúr-e f	keytureyó p
cattle	lólyo f	lolyeyó p (herds of-)
charcoal	jiláħ-e f	
cheek	gídam m	gidámme f (p)
——	ħaɖ m	ħàɖáɖ p
cheetah	doxóol m	doxoólle f (p)
chest	kac m	kàcác p
child	wéel m	
——, children	nyáxut m	
chin	ɖábal m	ɖabálle f (p)
centre	ɖáħ-e f	
circumcision	xándi m	
clan	gob m	gòbáb p
cloth	ɖafár-e f	ɖarfó p
cloud	míris m	mirísse f (p)
club	xóxom m	xoxómme f (p)
cobra	ráfle f	rafleyó p
coffee beans	bun m	
cold	rófo f	
colour	ɖoħ m	
comb	fílmac m	filmácce f (p)
container, big, water	ħaán-e f	ħáanán p
——, small, which the herders carry	soróor m	soroórre f (p)
——, milk	madál-e f	madaló p
——, milk	jíjo f	jijeyó p
——, milk	kúul m	kúulál p
——, milk	kuúni f	kuuniyó p

____ , to milk the camels	*urúub* m,	*uruúbbe* f (p)
____ , to keep fat	*udám-e* f,	*udamó* p
cooking stone	*kíndis* m,	*kindísse* f (p)
corpse	*gólfof* m,	*golfóffe* f (p)
cow	*sáħ-e* f,	*lólyo* f (p)
cowry, cowries	*elél-e* f	
crocodile	*yahási* m,	*yahasínye* f (p)
cup	*kókob* m,	*kokóbbe* f (p)
custom	*ħúgum* m,	*ħugúmme* f (p)
cutlass	*ilbánga* m,	*ilbangínye* f (p)
day	*sáħ-e* f	
____ , in counting	*ibéen* m (also night)	
____ , afternoon	*maalím-e* f (noon - 4 p.m.)	
desert	*ħeɖáɖ-e* f,	*ħeɖaɖó* p
dikdik	*sigáre* f	
dirt	*dúbsaH* m	
disease	*sigéer* m,	*sigeérre* f (p)
dog	*kar* m,	*kàrár* p
donkey	*éħel* m,	*eħél-e* f (p)
door	*afáf* p	
dowry	*gúnu* f	
draught	*nábħay* m	
dung, goats, camels	*jiróxo* f	
____ , cow	*úlul* m	
dust	*ebéer* m,	*ebeérre* f (p)
ear	*nabáħ-e* f,	*nabħó* p
____	*ɖóg-e* f	
ear, inside	*ħem* m	
earth	*íl-e* f	
egg	*ukáħ-e* f,	*ukaħó* p
elbow	*díkil* m,	*dikílle* f (p)
elder, married man	*maxábal* m,	*maxabálle* f (p)
elephant	*árab* m,	*aráb-e* f (p)
enclosure for animals	*sum* m,	*sùmám* p
enemy, enemies	*cíy-e* f	
evening	*geléb-e* f	*gelbó* p (4 - 7 p.m.)
		ħábe (7 - 10 p.m.)
eye	*íl-e* f,	*indó* p
eyelash(es)	*tírif* m	
face	*fol* m,	*fòlál* p
faeces	*údu* f	
family, unit	*éra* m,	*erínye* f (p)

——— ,	*gob* m,	*gòbáb* p
fat, camel	*tóm-e* f	
——— , from sheep's tail	*kárka* m	
——— , from soup	*énsi* f	
father	*ába* m,	*abínye* f (p)
——— , in law	*soyóoH* m	
feather	*túdub* m,	*tudúbbe* f (p)
female(s)	*deyóko* f	
fence	*oót-e* f	
fever	*árgab* m	
finger	*far* m,	*faró* p
fire	*dab* m,	*dàbáb* p (also rifle)
fireplace	*táf-e* f,	*tafó* p
firewood	*xóro* m,	*xorénye* f (p)
firstborn	*téyan* m,	*teyanó* p
flesh	*jid* m,	*jìdád* p
flower(s)	*bíx-e* f (also berry)	
fly, flies	*dakási* m	
——— , camelfly, flies	*dakár-e* f	
fog	*duubát* p	
food	*xoxáni* m	
———	*gólol* m	
foot, leg	*lúk-e* f,	*lukló* p
———	*danák-e* f,	*danakó* p
footprint	*sám-e* f,	*samó* p
forehead	*miín-e* f,	*miinó* p
forest	*omáar* m,	*omaárre* f (p)
frame to carry things	*séyney* m,	*seynéyye* f (p)
friend(s)	*al̠* m	
friend-bond	*deléy-e* f	
frog	*rak* m,	*rakó* p
garden	*gos* m,	*gòsás* p
gate of enclosure	*arít-e* f,	*artó* p
gift	*sím-e* f	
giraffe	*géri* m,	*gerínye* f (p)
girl	*inám-e* f	
——— , girls	*álbe* m	
——— , big, but unmarried	*galtáam* m,	*galtaám-e* f (p)
goats and sheep	*áddi* m	
goats	*ríy-e* f	
goats and sheep, young	*maxál-e* f	
——— , male, castrated	*túmay* m	
goat, male	*wákar* m,	*wakaró* p
——— , female	*wakár-e* f,	*wakaró* p

——, big male	*kéleH* m,	*keléH-e* f (p)
——, big female	*riḥíy-e* f,	*riyó* p
God	*wax* m	
gourd	*oróro* f,	*ororeyó* p
grass	*ḥós-e* f	
——, dry	*ḍum* m	
grandfather	*áci* m,	*acínye* f (p)
grandmother	*inkokó* f,	*inkokeyó* p
green	*úlaH* m	
ground	*il* m	
guest(s)	*márti* f	
gum	*ḥánja* f	
hair	*tím-e* f	
——, long	*ḥálḥal* m	
head	*mátaḥ* m,	*mataḥénye* f (p)
headrest	*loríga* f,	*lorigayó* p
heart	*rubéy-e* f,	*rubeyó* p
heel	*ḍádab* m,	*dadábbe* f (p)
hill	*kúr-e* f,	*kuró* p
hoe	*xóto* f,	*xoteyó* p
hole	*lum* m,	*lùmám* p
honey	*málab* m	
horn	*gáas* m,	*gaasó* p
——, snuf	*kúrum* m,	*kurúmme* f (p)
hospital	*síbtal* m,	*sibtálle* f (p)
house	*min* m,	*mìnán* p
——, small for old people	*rékey* m,	*rekéyye* f (p)
hump of camel	*gambár-e* f,	*gambaró* p
hunger	*ráraḥ* m	
——	*ánka* m	
husband	*áram* m,	*arámme* f (p)
hyena	*warába* m,	*warabénye* f (p)
ibis(es)	*yól-e* f	
impala	*ḥól-e* f	
injection	*írbi* m,	*irbínye* f(p)
inferiority	*dári* f	
intestines	*mindaxár-e* f	
iron	*bír-e* f	
jackal	*ḍowóḥo* f,	*ḍowoḥoyó* p
kidney	*kalási* f,	*kalasiyó* p
knee	*jílib* m,	*jilbó* p

⎯⎯	*kursánte* f,	*kursantiyó* p
knife	*warḥán-e* f,	*warḥanó* p
⎯⎯	*kinjér-e* f,	*kinjeró* p
lake	*béy-e* f,	*beyó* p
land	*il* m,	*ìlál* p
⎯⎯	*ḥárra* f	
⎯⎯ , medium dry	*xandíid* m	
⎯⎯ , uninhabited	*yib* m	
⎯⎯ , uninhabited	*dow* p	
language	*af* m,	*àfáf* p
law	*ámur* m	
leaf	*séeb* m,	*séebáb* p
leg	*lúḥ-e* f,	*luḥló* p
lid of container	*ínam* m,	*inámme* f (p)
lie	*beén-e* f,	*beenó* p
lightning	*anxáḍ* p	
lion	*baḥási* m	
lip	*furúr-e* f,	*fururó* p
liver	*ḥelési* f,	*ḥelesiyó* p
lizard(s)	*mulúḥ-e* f	
load(s)	*meḥ* m,	*mèḥáḥ* p
lungs	*sombób* p	
mais	*incabá* p	
male	*lab* m	
male(s)	*méjel* m	
man	*et* m	
man, men	*enyét* m	
marrow	*dóḥ-e* f	
mat, -roof	*dúlbe* m,	*dulbénye* f (p)
⎯⎯ , floor	*ílal* m,	*ilálle* f (p)
meat	*jiḍ* m,	*jìḍáḍ* p
⎯⎯ , fried	*galángal* m	
⎯⎯ , very fat	*ḥéḍ-e* f	
medicine man	*móro* f,	*moreyó* p
metal, tin	*gáḍar* m,	*gáḍarre* f (p)
mirror	*kitáab* m,	*kitaábbe* f (p)
milk, general	*ḥaanú* p	
⎯⎯ , different kinds mixed	*basbás* p	
⎯⎯ , mixture of fresh milk and blood	*benjó* p	
⎯⎯ , mixture of sour milk and blood	*soróy-e* f	
monkey(s)	*lacéer* m	
month	*ḥáy-e* f,	*ḥayó* p
moon	*yéyaH* m	

morning	*cirdér-e* f	
mother	*abár-e* f,	*arbó* p
mother, call name	*ayó*	
mother in law	*soyóoɦ* f	
mountain	*ɦal* m,	*ɦàlál* p
mouse	*uládu* m,	*uladinye* f (p)
mouth	*af* m,	*àfáf* p
mucus	*síim* m	
mud	*súb-e* f	
____, clay to make pots	*ɖóbo* f	
nail, claw	*gófan* m,	*gofánne* f (p)
name	*mágaɦ* m,	*magaɦénye* f (p)
navel	*ɦandúr-e* f,	*ɦanduró* p
neck	*luxúm-e* f,	*luxumó* p
necklace, general	*irtiyó* p	
____, of unmarried girl, red and white beads	*ariyó* p	
____, of married woman	*burgúrca* m	
____, of warrior	*inkéri* m	
needle	*írbi* m,	*irbínye* f (p)
news	*wor* m,	*wòrár* p
night	*ibéen* m,	*ibeénne* f (p)
nose	*sam* m,	*sàmám* p
nut	*xóna* f	
old people	*ewéen* m	
ostrich(es)	*nabáal* m	
outfit	*gaáɖ-e* f	
ox	*ɦéer* m,	*ɦéerár* p
palm of hand	*ɖanáɦ-e* f,	*ɖanaɦó* p
fan palm	*báar* m	
paper	*xadáab* m,	*xadaábbe* f (p)
peace	*nebéy-e* f	
penis	*gul* m,	*gùlál* p
people	*ényet* m	
____	*dod* m	
place	*meél-e* f,	*méelál* p
plain(s)	*tor* m,	*tòrár* p
plateau	*orrát-e* f,	*ortó* p
pot, clay	*díri* m,	*diriyó* p
proverb	*mamáɦ-e* f	
rabbit	*bakéla* m	
rain	*ɦir* m	

rainbow	*irtiyó* p	
rhinoceros	*wéjel* m,	*wejél-e* f (p)
rib	*wáru* m,	*warínye* f (p)
rich person	*kámur* m	
river	*ɦáw-e* f,	*ɦawó* p
road	*jit* m,	*jitát* p
rock	*líɦti* m,	*liɦtínye* f (p)
roof	*seréy-e* f (is 'sky')	
root	*ɦey* m,	*ɦèyáy* p
rope, in general	*yábar* m,	*yabárre* f (p)
——, made of camel skin	*daɦ* m,	*dàɦáɦ* p
——, made of camel skin	*gitím-e* f,	*gitimó* p
——, made of sisal	*yaráf-e* f	
——, camels wear around neck	*ɦérar* m,	*ɦerárre* f (p)
——, to tie small goats	*oróɦ-e* f	
rumor	*ɦam* m	
saliva	*ɦanjúf-e* f	
salt	*magád-e* f	
sand storm	*malálwa* m	
scar	*gúmar* m,	*gumárre* f (p)
scorpion(s)	*árar* m	
secretary bird(s)	*ingúbu* f	
seed	*ilím-e* f,	*ilmó* p
settlement	*gob* m,	*gòbáb* p
——, site	*urám-e* f	
——, former site	*ras* m,	*ràsás* p
——, very old site, abandoned long ago	*jébsi* m,	*jebsínye* f (p)
shadow	*osím-e* f,	*osimó* p
sheep and goats	*áddi* m	
——, young	*maxál-e* f	
sheep, in general	*iíy-e* f	
sheep, male	*ɦeléem* m,	*ɦelmó* p
——, female	*ɦeleém-e* f,	*ɦelmó* p
——, big male	*wárab* m,	*waráb-e* f (p)
——, big female	*láɦ-e* f,	*onó* p
——, female, which has not yet given birth	*subén-e* f,	*subenó* p
——, young male	*úrbor* m,	*urboró* p
——, young female	*urbór-e* f,	*urboró* p
——, (and goats) which have been castrated	*túmay* m	
shield	*gácam* m,	*gacámme* f (p)
shilling	*cílim* m,	*cilímme* f (p)
shoe	*kób-e* f,	*kobó* p
shoulder	*bárbar* m,	*barbárre* f (p)
sisal, wild	*éyma* f	

sister	*waláal* f,	*walalínye* f (p)
____ , elder	*índa* f	
skin	*gog* m,	*gògág* p
____ , prepared, camel	*maxéer* m,	*maxeérre* f (p)
____ , prepared, to wear	*sakál-e* f,	*sakaló* p
____ , prepared, cow, to sleep on	*níb-e* f,	*nibó* p
____ , prepared, goat	*útaH* m,	*uktó* p
sky	*seréy-e* f	
smoke	*um* m,	*ùmám* p
snake	*tóof* m,	*tóofáf* p
soil	*il* m	
soup	*cícax* m,	*cicáxxe* f (p)
spear	*tóor* m,	*tóorár* p
spider(s)	*árti* f	
spoon	*nyaráab* m,	*nyaraábbe* f (p)
squirrel(s)	*úres* m	
star	*bákal* m,	*bakálle* f (p)
____ ,	*yeyeħím-e* f	
stick	*láħaw* m,	*laħáw-e* f (p)
____ , big, bent, for building the house	*útub* m,	*utúbbe* f (p)
stomach	*ur* m,	*ùrár* p
stone	*ɖágaH* m,	*ɖagáH-e* f (p)
stool	*kombór-e* f,	*komboró* p
strength	*míg-e* f	
sun	*orráħ-e* f	
sweets	*nánaħ* m	
sword	*bírlab* m	*birlábbe* f (p)
tail, behind	*dub* m,	*dùbáb* p
tale	*ħáwes* m,	*ħawésse* f (p)
tear	*ilím-e* f,	*ilmó* p
termite(s)	*ririm-e* f	
thing	*waláħ* p	
thirst	*súgub* m	
thunder	*karkaraħó* p	
tick(s)	*cilím-e* f	
____ , big	*túrdac* m	
tin	*gádar* m,	*gadárre* f (p)
tobacco	*tómbo* f	
tongue	*ħárab* m,	*ħarábbe* f (p)
tool, iron	*lumát-e* f	
tooth	*iláH-e* f,	*ilkó* p
____ , molar	*góos* m,	*góosás* p
tortoise	*ɖíim* m,	*ɖíimám* p
tree	*gey* m,	*gèyó* p

tribe	*yáf-e* f,	*yafó* p
truth	*rúm-e* f	
turban	*dúub* m,	*dúubáb* p
tusk, elephant	*(h)ír-e* f,	*(h)ir(y)ó* p
twig	*sírbi* f,	*sirbiyó* p
twin, male	*mandáan* m,	*mandaanó* p
____, female	*mandaán-e* f,	*mandaanó* p
uncle, paternal	*abáya* m,	*abayínye* f (p)
____, maternal	*abíyo* m,	*aptínye* f (p)
urine	*káti* f	
vagina	*gel* m,	*gèlál* p
vein	*ħey* m,	*hèyáy* p
____, for bleeding	*ħam* m,	*ħàmám* p
viper	*ebésa* f,	*ebeseyó* p
voice	*ħoy* m,	*ħòyáy* p
vulture(s)	*rad* m	
wall	*bórox* m	
war	*ɖíħo* f	
warriors	*ħeér-e* f (p)	
wart	*cilmám-e* f,	*cilmamó* p
water	*bicé* p	
water hole, big	*gátab* m,	*gatábbe* f (p)
____, small	*ħár-e* f,	*ħaró* p
____, deep	*giɖím-e* f,	*giɖimó* p
week	*téyba* f,	*teybeyó* p
well	*wór-e* f,	*woró* p
widow	*múnxo* f	
wife	*arám-e* f,	
wind	*ħáfar* m	
____, cold	*táfuf* m	
window	*dóħ-e* f,	*doħó* p
wing	*bárbar* m,	*bárbarre* f (p)
woman	*maxabál-e* f	
women, wives	*obórri* m	
worm	*déyaħ* m	
wound	*jis* m,	*jìsás* p
year	*gu(h)* m,	*gù(h)á(h)* p
yellow, of camels	*sóri* f,	*soriyó* p
____, of rainbow	*dárle* f	

REFERENCES

Abraham, R.C.
    1964.   *Somali-English Dictionary.* London: University of London Press.

Almkvist, H.
    1881.   *Die Bischari-Sprache.* Upsala.

Andrzejewski, B.W.
    1960.   "The categories of number in noun forms in the Borana dialect of Galla." *Africa*
                 30:62-75.

    1964.   *The Declensions of Somali Nouns.* London: School of Oriental and African Studies.

Armstrong, L.
    1934.   "The phonetic structure of Somali." *Mitteilungen des Seminars fur Orientalischen*
                 Sprachen zu Berlin 37 (3):116-61.

Bell, C.R.V.
    1953.   *The Somali Language.* London: Longmans, Green & Co.

Black, P.D.
    1974.   "Lowland East Cushitic, subgrouping and reconstruction." Ph.D. Dissertation,
                 Yale University.

Castellino, G.R.
    1975.   "Gender in Cushitic." In *Hamito-Semitica,* ed. J. and T. Bynon, pp. 333-59. The
                 Hague: Mouton.

Colizza, G.
    1887.   *Lingua 'Afar del nord-est dell'Africa,* Vienna.

Fleming, H.C.
    1964.   "Baiso and Rendille, Somali outliers." *Rassegna di Studi Etiopici* 20:35-96.

Greenberg, J.H.
    1963.   "Some universals of grammar with particular reference to the order of meaningful
                 elements." In *Universals of Language*, ed. J.H. Greenberg, pp. 73-113. Cambridge,
                 Mass.: MIT press.

Hayward, R.J.
    1978.   "Bayso revisited: some preliminary linguistic observations 1." *BSOAS* 41:539-70.

    1979.   "Bayso revisited: some preliminary linguistic observations 2." *BSOAS* 42:101-132.

Heine, B.
    1975/76a.   "Notes on the Rendille Language (Kenya)." *Afrika und Ubersee* 59:176-223.

1975/76b.   "Bemerkungen zur Elmolo Sprache." *Afrika und Ubersee* 59:278-99.

1976/77.   "Bemerkungen zur Boni Sprache (Kenya)." *Afrika und Ubersee* 60:242-95.

Hetzron, R.
1967.   "Agaw Numerals and Incongruence in Semitic." *Journal of Semitic Studies* 12:169-97.

1972.   "Phonology in Syntax." *Journal of Linguistics* 8:251-65.

1976.   "The Agaw Languages." *Afroasiatic Linguistics* 3 (3):1-40.

Hudson, Grover.
1976.   "Highland East Cushitic." In *The Non-Semitic Languages of Ethiopia*, ed. M.L. Bender, pp. 232-77. Michigan: Michigan State University.

Hudson, Richard A.
1973.   "Syllables, mora's and accents in Beja." *Journal of Linguistics* 9:53-63.

McCawley, J.D.
1968.   *The Phonological Component of a Grammar of Japanese.* The Hague: Mouton.

Moreno, M.M.
1940.   *Manuale di Sidamo.* Rome: A.Mondadori.

Newman, Paul.
1972.   "Syllable weight as a phonological variable." *Studies in African Linguistics* 3:301-23.

Oomen, A.
1978.   "Focus in the Rendille clause." *Studies in African Linguistics* 9:35-65.

Pike, Eunice.
1974.   "A multiple stress system versus a tone system." *International Journal of American Linguistics* 40:169-75.

Sasse, H.-J.
1974.   "Notes on the structure of Galab." *BSOAS* 37:407-38.

Schlee, G.
1978.   *Sprachliche Studien zum Rendille.* Hamburger philologische Studien, 46. Hamburg: Helmut Buske.

von Tiling, M.
1921/22.   "Die Sprache der Jabarti." *Zeitschrift fur Eingeborenen Sprachen* 12:17-52, 97-162.

Tucker, A.N. and M.A. Bryan.
1956.   *The Non-Bantu Languages of North Eastern Africa, Part 3.* London: IAI.